Japan's Market

Japan's Market:
The Distribution System

by
Michael R. Czinkota
and
Jon Woronoff

PRAEGER

PRAEGER SPECIAL STUDIES • PRAEGER SCIENTIFIC

New York • Westport, Connecticut • London

Library of Congress Cataloging-in-Publication Data

Czinkota, Michael R.
  Japan's market.

  "Praeger special studies. Praeger scientific."
  Bibliography: p.
  Includes index.
  1. Marketing channels — Japan. I. Woronoff, Jon.
II. Title.
HF5415.129.C95   1986   381'.0952   86-8157
ISBN 0-275-92142-5 (alk. paper)

Library of Congress Catalog Card Number: 86-8157
ISBN: 0-275-92142-5

First published in 1986

Praeger Publishers, 521 Fifth Avenue, New York, NY 10175
A division of Greenwood Press, Inc.

Printed in the United States of America

The paper used in this book complies with the Permanent
Paper Standard issued by the National Information Standards
Organization (Z39.48-1984).

10 9 8 7 6 5 4 3 2 1

9004754

To our wives

Foreword

Michael Czinkota and Jon Woronoff have done an excellent job of documenting the intricacies of the Japanese distribution system. As such, the book provides valuable insights for U.S. firms seeking to do business in Japan. It is also a helpful reference for U.S. trade negotiators and policymakers in their efforts to develop the best strategies for increasing our exports to Japan.

The authors note that the U.S. has negotiated intensely with Japan on problems of market access with only limited success when measured on a standard of increased sales. In their view, because of the restrictiveness of the Japanese distribution system, the U.S. would have difficulty penetrating the Japanese market even if all the current negotiating efforts to eliminate specific barriers were successful.

The principal purposes of the book are to (1) let outsiders know how the Japanese distribution system functions, and (2) provide suggestions to foreign companies on how to operate within the system. The book contains separate chapters on the grouping of businesses known as *keiretsu*, on the retail sector, and on the wholesale sector. Each chapter describes the historical evolution, current functioning, and trends for the future of the topic under discussion. Each chapter also contains advice to foreign businesses on how to get around the constraints of the Japanese market.

The restrictiveness of the distribution system results from two factors: (1) its complex nature, and (2) the close relationship among Japanese business groups which tend not to purchase from outside suppliers. The authors point out that Japanese business decisions often are based on historical traditions of loyalty and stability. A manufacturer will channel his goods exclusively through one wholesaler, for example. He may offer financing and other services to aid the wholesaler's business. The wholesaler in turn will not sell competing goods. The book notes that business groupings often develop an insider/outsider mentality. They get used to doing business almost entirely with a group of related firms.

These aspects of Japanese business have evolved gradually in a cultural context; they cannot be easily changed. The authors note that in some cases these traditional ties are loosening, which will make foreign entry easier. The authors believe that in most cases the Japanese distribution system has served its market well and that, where necessary, changes are taking place, albeit at a slow pace.

Some options for foreign firms that want to sell to the Japanese are outlined in a chapter called "Beating the System." The book explores the pros and cons of licensing, joint ventures, and setting up direct production. The authors state that the Japanese market is difficult to penetrate, but is not completely closed. Foreigners need to recognize how the system functions, and learn to succeed despite the constraints; a few U.S. firms have done so. The authors note that most of the advice is not relevant to small firms. Success in the Japanese market requires a long and expensive commitment to setting up a system for selling goods. The foreign firms with the best opportunities tend to be the biggest, most technologically advanced, and best financed.

The concluding chapter, titled "Toward a Level Playing Field," discusses steps that both the Japanese and U.S. public and private sectors can take to enhance U.S.-Japanese economic relations. The authors are optimistic that some changes are underway which will facilitate foreign sales in Japan. They cite as one example the increasing development of chain stores.

The private sector in Japan is facing an import imperative; if Japanese firms expect to retain the international market access from which they have so throughtly benefited, they must clearly be willing to reciprocate. Japanese businessmen should consider the internatonal trade implications of any domestic business decision. This advice of course applies also to U.S. businessmen, who wish to compete in world market, including Japan.

This comprehensive description of the Japanese business system should help U.S. businesses increase their sales to Japan. *Japan's Markets: The Distribution System* should be read by U.S. firms that want to sell a new product in the Japanese market. It is also useful for U.S. trade negotiators to keep in mind how the Japanese economy operates, in order to get the best possible results from our trade negotiating efforts.

William E. Brock
U.S. Secretary of Labor

Acknowledgments

Many individuals and institutions assisted the authors in their research for this book. Special thanks are owed to the Japanese Ministry of International Trade and Industry (MITI) and the Japan External Trade Organization (JETRO) for scheduling meetings and facilitating our work in Japan. The Office of the U.S. Trade Representative and the U.S. Department of Commerce provided vital input and additional perspectives. The Distribution Systems Research Institute supported our research through funding, arranging interviews, and gathering data. The authors also extend their gratitude to the many firms, managers, government officials, and researchers, both in the United States and Japan, who participated in the interviews and prepared crucial materials.

Special mention is owed to Mr. Robert Conkling of Global USA, Dr. Bernard J. LaLonde of the Ohio State University, Mr. Steven R. Saunders of Saunders and Company, and Dr. Neil C. Livingstone for all their helpful comments. We are also grateful to Dodwell Marketing Consultants in Tokyo, who kindly granted us permission to reprint materials from their publications. The manuscript was edited and typed by Ms. Anne Talbot and Mr. Richard Farano, both of the National Center for Export-Import Studies. Our thanks go to all of them. Any errors of omission or commission are, of course, the responsibility of the authors.

Contents

List Of Tables And Figures

TABLES

FIGURES

Part I
FACING THE ULTIMATE BARRIERS

1
Focus On The Japanese Market

International commerce should, or so the theory goes, contribute to international understanding and mutual prosperity. Yet, at least as concerns the relations between Japan and its partners, the result has been constantly growing friction and endless rounds of recrimination about who is getting the most out of trade.

Trade conflicts have existed in one form or another for over two decades. Initially, this conflict was restricted to specific sectors where Japan sold too much and hurt domestic industries. It has since spread and become more general as Japan's trade surpluses grew. From concern with Japanese exports, the conflict has shifted increasingly to annoyance at not being able to coax Japan into importing more. The situation was already unpleasant during the 1960s and 1970s when trade was still growing nicely; it has become more painful in a time of relative stagnation.

In a world economy where it is hard to make both ends meet, it is irritating to find that one country has been doing so well. Aside from two brief periods after the first and second oil crises in 1973 and 1979, Japan has run a positive trade balance. Indeed, the balance almost exploded in recent years, starting with a modest $5 billion surplus in 1981.[1] By fiscal 1983, it had reached a record high of $23 billion, only to be exceeded by another record surplus of $35 billion in 1984. Most forecasts, both Japanese and foreign, predict that the trade surpluses will continue swelling in coming years and, indeed, indefinitely.

Large and expanding Japanese surpluses naturally reflect large and expanding deficits of other countries. The United States suffered a record deficit of $21 billion in fiscal 1983, followed by another, more disastrous, deficit of $34 billion in 1984. But it was not alone. The European Community ran a deficit of $10 billion in 1984, and East Asia as a whole (ASEAN, China, and the "newly industrialized countries") ran a $7 billion deficit in the same year. Deficits occurred in other places, including Africa and Latin America. For them as well, forecasts indicated more deficits to come unless something arrested the trend.

The deficits inevitably focused attention on both sides of the trade equation. The situation for Japan's exports was quite clear. Its manufacturers produced goods of excellent quality at reasonable prices that were welcomed by consumers the world over. It was easy for Japanese companies to get into most markets and sell directly or through the existing channels. Their success was shown by booming sales and rising market shares—and often by trade friction and surpluses.[2]

This provoked a negative reaction abroad, but one that was partly understandable and bound to intensify if nothing corrected the imbalances. It took the form of an increasing number of trade barriers to protect endangered domestic industries such as textiles, steel, shipbuilding, automobiles, and electronics. Soon there were broader demands for protectionism in many circles. While the principle of free trade was not renounced, it was certainly infringed upon more and more.[3]

The other side of the equation was not as readily perceptible. It was maintained by foreign companies that they also offered good products at reasonable prices and that more of them should be sold in Japan. Such claims were made at both ends of the spectrum, among high-tech firms in advanced countries and simpler ones in developing nations whose labor costs were very low. All of the companies had been able to sell their goods in international markets and often competed successfully against Japanese goods in third countries. Yet whenever they tried to enter the Japanese market, they encountered exceptional difficulties and made little headway.[4]

This failure to penetrate was reflected in the trade statistics. Japan imported proportionately less manufactures than other countries at the same economic level. The share of manufactured imports in total imports was a mere 26 percent in 1979 as opposed to 58 percent for the United States and 62 percent for the European Community. At the same time, the ratio of manufactured imports to gross domestic product only amounted to some 2 percent, half the U.S. level. These figures have remained amazingly constant over the past decades, actually falling after the oil crisis, only to return slowly to the original mark.[5]

Within these imports, which were less than exports, and within the manufactured goods, which were at lower levels than other advanced countries, there was a third anomaly. The share of consumer goods was a mere 20 percent and sometimes less. Most other manufactures were either capital goods or intermediate goods, namely products that helped Japan generate its own finished products and machinery. This meant that the outlook for future progress was bleak since Japanese companies were still gearing up to replace imported articles.

It therefore became urgent to seek the causes of this inability to sell more goods in general, and more manufactured (and especially consumer) goods in particular. In so doing, its partners finally realized that Japan had also been protecting its market, not always in the same ways but certainly using methods that were equally effective. Indeed, on closer inspection it appeared to many that Japan had the most closed and impenetrable market of them all. This was steadfastly denied by the government and business leaders, but it was evident that barriers were present and had to be eliminated to facilitate access.

NOTES

1. Ministry of Finance. Japanese trade statistics are on a customs-clearance basis and do not always coincide with comparable figures collected by its various trading partners.

2. See I. M. Destler and Hideo Sato, eds., *Coping with U.S.–Japanese Economic Conflicts*, D. C. Heath, Lexington, 1982, and Jon Woronoff, *World Trade War*, Praeger, New York, 1984, pp. 108–84.

3. See Woronoff, op. cit., pp. 218–55.

4. Ibid., pp. 55-107.

5. See Sumihiko Seto, "Manufactured Imports and their Marketing Promotion Strategies," *The Wheel Extended*, Summer, 1980, pp. 2–5.

2

Impediments, Ordinary

When foreign business executives and governments began seeking the causes of their difficulties in penetrating the Japanese market, there was no shortage of impediments to be found.[1] In fact, it soon turned out that there were several different levels of difficulties. It was rare that just one obstacle had to be overcome. Behind it was another, and often yet another. The comparisons most often made were to speak of the layers of an onion or a castle with its surrounding fortifications.

The outside layer or external fortification was the rather common and conventional one of tariffs and quotas. After the war, Japanese industry had grown up behind a whole battery of such mechanisms. Even in the mid-1960s the effective customs tariff rate was as much as 21 percent. This was considerably higher than in other advanced countries at the time. The number of import restrictions was also substantial, 50 for manufactured goods and 60 for agricultural goods.

Gradually, these conventional barriers were brought down. But, like its counterparts, the Japanese government was selective so that those that had little practical purpose were reduced first while others were preserved until the bitter end. This left towering peaks even when the general level was much lower.[2]

Examples of selective protection included the automotive industry, where the abolition of quotas on passenger cars came only in 1966, at which time the tariffs remained as high as 35 to 40 percent. Long after tariffs on computers were reduced, those for peripherals stayed high. This effort to protect such major industries was more understandable than some others. The tariffs on confectionaries, alcoholic beverages, and processed foods are still inexplicably high. Even now there are strict quotas on leather and leather footwear.

Behind the tariffs and quotas—sometimes already in place, sometimes raised as the former came down—were the nontariff barriers (NTBs). This sort of impediment is in place in just about every trading nation. But NTBs have never taken on such a varied and ingenious nature, applying to just about any product under the sun, nor were they ever more prolific than they are in Japan.[3]

Those NTBs that had the most defensible basis were related to product and health safety. They were particularly dense in the sectors of foodstuffs and pharmaceuticals.[4] But NTBs often seemed to exceed any reasonable bounds. For example, in addition to clinical retesting of new drugs, it was necessary to repeat the preclinical testing in Japan. This meant tests that are normally run on white mice in laboratories had to be redone at great cost in time and money. Even more frivolous was the requirement that mineral water be pasteurized by heating.[5]

While the safety requirements often made sense, the procedures were unnecessarily complicated. It was obligatory to test exceptionally large numbers, for exceptionally long times, under exceptionally arduous conditions. Test certificates already obtained from national authorities were not accepted, and thus the whole process had to be repeated. It was not possible to have the testing done locally; it had to be done after the goods arrived in Japan. In some cases, every single article (for example, each individual car) had to be tested. Things dragged on further because inspectors were too few or too slow.

For goods where standards were applicable, often the Japanese standards favored domestic manufacturers. It was necessary to use the same techniques and design when others were equally effective. Some of the requirements were petty and obviously biased against competing foreign products, especially those concerning size, weight, or material. This included regulations that made it hard to sell foreign lumber or plywood.

What was worse, the standards were sometimes modified at very short notice . . . for foreigners at least. It therefore turned out that a product that had been sold on the Japanese market was no longer acceptable.[6] Even more absurd, when a product was improved it had to undergo all the formalities and testing another time and could not be sold until they were completed. Finally, the certificates of approval were usually given to the local agent and not the foreign manufacturer—and if the agent changed, the manufacturer had to go through the whole process all over again.

In addition to bone fide standards—which at least were on paper—there were many others that were imparted by verbal suggestions of the local officials in the form of "administrative guidance." These were usually unclear and so at times were disclosed only to domestic manufacturers. Foreigners were then expected to meet conditions that had never been explained to them and could be found in no book. The most striking case of this was a limitation on the ingredients that could be used for cosmetics, only some of which were indicated to foreigners while many more were known and used by Japanese. Also, while not compulsory, it was helpful for goods to bear supposed quality marks like JAS and SG, which few foreign products could obtain.

Government officials and bureaucrats imposed many other handicaps.[7] Customs inspectors tended to be overly meticulous in checking whether imported goods met all the conditions. This could take the form of time-consuming checks in which the slightest, inconsequential failing could result in rejection. What was particularly unpleasant was that it was impossible to get a ruling as to why a rejection occurred; often goods rejected at one point might be cleared at another point.

Other forms of bureaucratic intervention were unique to and exceedingly important in the Japanese context. Some arose from the practice of industrial policy and targeting by certain ministries. In this, the ministry would provide specific incentives and broad support to local companies, which put them at an advantage over foreign competitors. This included all sorts of tax rebates, accelerated depreciation of equipment, aid in acquiring technologies and raw materials, and so on. Another aspect was research and development carried out by public bodies and then put at the disposal of selected manufacturers. The best known examples were to upgrade the quality of Japanese computers.

In addition to support, however, there was also protection. As soon as it was determined to promote an "infant industry," barriers went up to preserve the market until demand could be met by local companies. This protection included tariffs, quotas, and NTBs and was supplemented by government or other purchases. Only after the industry could fend for itself was most of the protection removed—but it could be restored if the sector encountered difficulties or went into a decline. Measures for ailing industries involved cartels and other means for restricting competing imports.

Industrial policy has been practiced most systematically by the Ministry of International Trade and Industry (MITI) for a broad range of sectors. Its role was substantial earlier on for coal, iron and steel, light metals, chemicals and petrochemicals, automobiles, electronics, and computers. Nowadays it backs biotechnology, new materials, atomic energy, and aerospace. But MITI is not the only example. Similar activities are undertaken by the Ministry of Health to promote the pharmaceutical and medical equipment industries; the Ministry of Agriculture cultivates the farm machinery sector even more strongly; the Science and Technology Agency helps some high-tech areas; and so on.

From the outset, the government engaged in a "buy Japan" policy that was not so different from the analogous policies abroad. Yet, even after rules on opening procurement were adopted, the government was slow to enforce them. Local governments tended to overlook these agreements, and semigovernmental agencies regularly ignored them. This included the Japanese National Railways (JNR), the Tobacco Monopoly, and especially Nippon Telegraph and Telephone (NTT).

The amounts of money involved here were tremendous. Even more significant was the way contracting occurred on the basis of negotiated prices rather than open bidding. This made it possible to help a company launch a product by guaranteeing a market. This was done most extensively for telecommunications equipment and computers by NTT. JNR obtained its rolling stock locally even when competitive goods existed abroad. The most extreme case was, of course, to create a domestic cigarette industry that could flourish only in the absence of imports.

As periodically noted, none of the barriers or measures were unknown abroad. But they were never as extensive or as deeply embedded, nor as effective in blocking imports. And they also remained in place long after other countries had liberalized.

NOTES

1. American Chamber of Commerce in Japan, *Report on Trade Barriers, Membership Survey*, Tokyo, 1982.

2. See Michael Blaker, ed., *The Politics of Trade: US and Japanese Policy Making for the GATT Negotiations*, Columbia University Press, New York, 1978.

3. Arthur D. Little, *The Japanese Non-Tariff Barrier Issue*, Tokyo, 1979.

4. Kearney International, *Non-Tariff Barriers Affecting the Health Care Industry in Japan*, Tokyo, 1980.

5. For an analysis of nontariff barriers in the pharmaceutical, cosmetics, foodstuffs, and automotive industries, see Jon Woronoff, *Inside Japan, Inc.*, Lotus Press, Tokyo, 1982, pp. 131–65.

6. Frank A. Weil and Norman D. Glick, "Japan—Is the Market Open?" *Law and Policy in International Business*, Vol. 11, No. 3, 1979.

7. American Chamber of Commerce in Japan, op. cit.

3

Getting In Step

Slowly but surely, each of the layers was removed from the onion or the fortifications were battered down, depending on the preferred metaphor. But it was a long, drawn-out process that has now been going on for over two decades, although that is frequently forgotten. It has passed through several spurts of activity, with the first big push coming in the mid-1960s, a second in the late 1970s, and a third at present.

Shortly after the war, it was felt that Japan might not be able to rebuild and become a modern industrial economy again. Japan was therefore allowed to adopt rather stringent measures to that end, and its use of "infant industry" protection was initially accepted. It was even tolerated much later as the country began to expand and export. Only when its exports became irksome was it realized that Japan had outgrown the old methods and should be held to the same conduct as other advanced countries. This decision was consecrated by Japan's acceptance of Article VIII of the International Monetary Fund and entry in the Organization for Economic Cooperation and Development and the General Agreement on Tariffs and Trade (GATT) as of 1963.

This initiated a series of moves that was reinforced by the Kennedy Round of multilateral trade negotiations of 1964–67. Customs tariffs fell sharply from 21 percent in 1966, to 10 percent in 1973, and to 5 percent in 1974, which was comparable to other advanced nations.[1] The average dropped further in the early 1980s, thanks to the Tokyo Round and special efforts to accelerate its implementation. By now, Japan's level is much lower than that of the United States or of the European Community.

The same process occurred for quotas. There were as many as 460 import restrictions in 1962. By the end of the decade this had decreased to 110. In 1975 most were discarded and only 27 residual items remain, of which just five were for manufactured goods. But it has been hard to remove the last few despite strong urging from abroad. In its defense, Japan can point out that most European countries are far worse.

The struggle to eliminate nontariff barriers made little progress until the early 1980s, although individual business executives or working parties like the U.S.–Japan Trade Study Group revealed their presence and unfairness. It was only the growing trade imbalances and ensuing friction that led the governments to tackle these more intricate and delicate items—which were more visible than ever now that many tariffs had come down. Unlike the situation with GATT for tariffs and quotas, there was no suitable machinery to deal with NTBs. This meant that Japan's trading partners could do little more than complain and threaten. This ultimately proved effective, as Japan was dependent on trade and eager to demonstrate its cooperativeness.

For a long time, the very existence of NTBs was strenuously denied by the Japanese government. Then, in 1982, there was a breakthrough. The Esaki Committee, appointed by the Liberal Democratic Party, examined 99 alleged NTBs and conceded that 67 of them did exist. Gradually, the government was forced to admit that there were considerably more. It was aided in this task of uncovering NTBs by foreign businesses, which now felt freer to express their grievances.

Thus, during the 1980s, NTBs were painstakingly removed, one after the other, although some new ones cropped up. Even more important, it was recognized that broader measures had to be taken as well. It was necessary to increase the transparency of the standard-setting exercise so that outsiders would know exactly what the standards were in good time. Indeed, on occasion they might participate in bodies that set these standards. Foreigners could also receive certain quality marks, and more foreign data and tests could be accepted while additional inspectors were posted abroad.

Government ministries and agencies were also called on to make things clearer and simpler for foreign businesses. To solve any possible problems, a special Office of the Trade Ombudsman was set up to receive complaints and look into their justification. It could coordinate the efforts of all other bodies so that any difficulties might be quickly overcome. The individual administrations also provided more help and advice than before. While much remained to be done, the bureaucracy did become somewhat more responsive.

Government procurement was progressively opened at both the central and local levels, although not as much or as rapidly as had been hoped.[2] Much more promising, the semigovernmental agencies that had the biggest budgets and had been most difficult in the past were undergoing privatization. It was assumed that, once subject to market forces, they would have to buy the best and cheapest goods available. This occurred first with the Tobacco Monopoly and Nippon Telegraph and Telephone. The Japanese National Railways was slated for later privatization.

Meanwhile, industrial policy had become almost an embarrassment to the Japanese government, which tried not to engage in spectacular R & D projects or, if so, to see that some foreign companies participated.[3] More generally, there were relatively fewer new industries to be promoted by MITI or other bodies, although there is no doubt that aerospace enjoys some protection and sales of foreign satellites and rockets are hurt. Where the most serious problems remain are with regard to the ailing industries that are still supported by MITI, including aluminum, pulp and paper, and petrochemicals.

While most of these advances were piecemeal, they were presented within the framework of a series of "market-opening" packages, which were adopted by the government with much fanfare. They included further reductions in tariffs (although not suppression of quotas), fairer standards and inspection, greater procurement of foreign goods, more transparency in government action, and so on. No less than six such packages were introduced between 1981 and 1985, the last being the most impressive. This "action program" of Prime Minister Nakasone was to be implemented over a period of three years. By 1988, or so it was presumed, there should be no further grounds for complaint.

Alas, while the improvements were highly appreciated, none of the market-opening packages aroused much enthusiasm in foreign business or government circles. In fact, Nakasone's program was criticized as inadequate by foreign observers; the U.S. government representative even spoke of "deep disappointment."[4] Republican Senator John Heinz went yet further: "Japan has announced five previous market-opening initiatives in the past four years. None of them has worked. That's the reason for this sixth initiative. I doubt this will do much good either."[5]

The causes for doubt or dissatisfaction were many. One was that the measures were again selective, often liberalizing sectors of scant importance and protecting others that were more essential. Then, the implementation was questionable. Some promises remained purely verbal because no machinery was created to put them into practice. In other cases, it was clear that even if there were a formal commitment at higher levels, there was a lack of goodwill further down among the ordinary bureaucrats who had to carry the measures out. And, of course, it was repeatedly lamented that old barriers were simply replaced by new ones.

Increasingly, commentators insisted that the "proof of the pudding is in the eating." This signified that the only way of showing that the liberalization was meaningful was for the trade situation to change dramatically, namely, for many more foreign products to be sold to Japan. Alas, there was little evidence that things were improving in this sense. The share of manufactured imports remained stable and imports expanded much less rapidly than exports. Trade imbalances not only remained large, they grew implacably. And most forecasts indicated even more bloated imbalances to come.

In a sense, it was unfair to demand that the measures be translated into concrete sales. It might be that foreign companies did not supply products that were good and cheap enough to get into the market, or they did not make the requisite marketing efforts. These points were ritually made by Japanese representatives—and very poorly taken by their foreign counterparts.

Fair or not, it was clear that the conflicts could not be resolved until more exports were successful and the Japanese market actually did absorb foreign goods, improving both the trade balance and political relations.

NOTES

1. *KKC Brief No. 29*, Tokyo, Keizai Roho Center, July, 1985.
2. Chikara Higashi, *Japanese Trade Policy Formulation*, Praeger, New York, 1983, pp. 106–14.
3. Ministry of International Trade and Industry, *Background Information on Japan's Industrial Policy*, May, 1983.
4. *Daily Yomiuri*, June 28, 1985, p. 1.
5. *Time*, July 1, 1985.

4

Impediments, Extraordinary

It slowly dawned on most observers that the reason things were not improving was not so much that goods were blocked by a series of impediments: tariffs and quotas, nontariff barriers and bureaucratic hassles, government procurement and industrial policy. It was not that the market-opening measures were poorly implemented or partially counteracted. It was not even that Japanese goods were so superior that foreign ones could not compete. It was that further, uncharted barriers remained.

After peeling away all the layers, after taking all the outlying fortifications, there was still something more. This something was never clearly articulated or accurately grasped, but it was becoming increasingly evident that the place to look was in the distribution system. Here, there were two primary elements that had to be taken into account: the complex and unwieldly nature of the system itself, and the special relationships that arose between various agents in the distribution process.

Foreign businesses in Japan had long been aware of these problems, and occasionally complained to their governments. But it took some time for the politicians and bureaucrats to realize just how important such barriers could be. Eventually they grasped that it was impossible to sell even the finest goods if they could not get on the store shelves or into the display rooms. And it served little purpose to dismantle tariffs and quotas, NTBs and red tape, government procurement and the rest if special relationships between local businesses discouraged imports.

Still, in 1982 the U.S. Department of Commerce did list the distribution system among the obstacles to trade. In particular, it pointed out that it could be considered a "non-tariff barrier to imports." The difficulties derived "from a complex, somewhat archaic system that, particularly with regard to consumer goods, evolved over time to meet the particular needs of the domestic market. Criticism of the Japanese distribution system often focuses on the very high retail prices of imported goods." Awareness of the role of intercompany relations was more nebulous. It was merely noted that "cartel-like activity among Japanese firms can limit access to distribution channels."[1]

Once again, the Japanese authorities—governmental and especially business—denied any such barriers or disadvantages for foreign traders. They were pointedly dismissed in a recent statement of the Japan Federation of Econonic Organizations (Keidanren), the principal voice of the business community:

"The myth persists that business relations in Japan are fixed and unchanging, that transactions among members of a group predominate, and that the market is difficult to penetrate, even with superior products to offer. In fact, however, intragroup business deals are not common. The Japanese market is simply too competitive to allow success based on dependence on special trading relationships. There is also loud criticism of the Japanese distribution system, but studies have made it clear that, while much room remains for improvement, the system itself does not discriminate against foreign goods."[2]

Yet, some of the complaints were hard to refute. Even the Economic Planning Agency had to admit the complications of the distribution system. A 1984 report indicated that the distribution routes were more than three times longer than in the United States and Europe, and the productivity per employee in the wholesale and retail sectors was only two-thirds that of the United States.[3] Numerous polls showed that consumers regarded the prices of imported goods as excessively high, and there was no doubt that multilayered channels and large margins accounted for some of that.[4] Also, the activities of the major industrial groups and keiretsu were a basic fact of business life.

Thus, it was obvious that something had to be done. But what? Most of the distribution and other commercial arrangements were traditional and had become an integral part of the economic scene. It would be most difficult to change them effectively and, with some justice, the Japanese insisted that they had a right to their own business culture. The financial connections, on the other hand, were frequently more important than any customs and practices and were occasionally of a dubious nature. To the extent that this did discriminate against their nationals, foreign governments might feel compelled to complain or exert political pressure. But there was little more they could do since none of this came under GATT or other international agreements.

Perhaps conceding the difficulty of entering the market, the Japanese government did attempt to ease the process in certain ways. As of the early 1980s, it launched "buy foreign" campaigns. Special "import fairs" were held in which foreign products would be displayed in varous parts of Japan. "Import-buying missions" were sent abroad to purchase foreign goods. The most spectacular gesture by Prime Minister Nakasone when presenting his "action program" was to make a special appeal to the Japanese public to buy more foreign articles. MITI subsequently asked the major companies to set ambitious targets for imports.

But this could be of only secondary use. The import missions purchased only limited quantities of goods. The fairs introduced products to the market but did nothing to facilitate their passage through the existing channels. The Japanese became benevolent importers, whereas what was needed was to enable foreign companies to export more of their goods normally.

Thus, the distribution system contains the ultimate and most decisive barriers. Although some aspects are undergoing change and some difficulties are being overcome, it is still very difficult for foreigners to operate in the Japanese structure. To improve the situation, it is essential to know much more about how the distribution channels and corporate groups function.

The purpose of this book is to describe the situation in these two essential areas. First, the various groupings and special relationships that tie distributors to manufacturers and bind manufacturers among themselves are explored. Then the wholesale and retail sectors are carefully examined. In both cases, the structures as well as the operations are studied so that outsiders may understand how they work. Since the system is presently undergoing considerable evolution, the changes that have occurred so far are indicated and prospects for further change elucidated. Last, but certainly not least, the authors provide useful pointers on how foreign companies can function within the system and where the best opportunities lie.

NOTES

1. United States Congress, *Hearings before the Committee on Foreign Affairs, House of Representatives*, March-August, 1982, Washington, D.C., Government Printing Office.

2. *KKC Brief No. 26*, Tokyo, Keizai Koho Center, February, 1985, p. 1.

3. *Japan Economic Journal*, June 26, 1984.

4. *Daily Yomiuri*, "Imported Goods Still Dear; Consumers Balk," April 15, 1985, p. 2.

Part II
A MOST
ORGANIZED MARKET

5

The Inescapable Groupings

It can hardly be stressed enough that every business community has its own characteristic features. Some commercial practices and legal institutions encountered in one place may not be found, or appear only in a somewhat different form, elsewhere. Others that are generally lacking abroad may be of particular significance in a specific country. Given its lengthy autonomous growth remote from Western culture and its periodic phases of isolation and nationalism, it is hardly surprising that the differences in Japan should be notable despite any real or apparent resemblance to the West.

One of the most striking differences, when properly understood, is the extent to which markets are organized and structured in certain ways by units that are sometimes called *keiretsu*, if more formal, and merely groups or groupings if less so. These are "alignments" or combinations of companies, more or less closely related and coordinated, that do business with one another on a regular—and often quite intimate—basis.

Three basic categories of groupings should be carefully considered. One is the more traditional type, which is most frequently called *keiretsu*, and consists of a number of companies in diverse sectors that revolve around one of the leading banks. This is often referred to as a horizontal grouping. Another derives from the supplier networks created by dynamic manufacturers, commonly known as a vertical grouping. The third is referred to as a distribution *keiretsu* since it brings together a manufacturer and its sales outlets.

These various groupings play an extremely important role in the Japanese economy. It is hardly possible to do business in Japan, as a local or foreign entity, without running into them as buyers or sellers, clients or suppliers, friends or competitors. Yet their formation, organization, and activities have been inadequately explored in the literature and, what is worse, poorly grasped by those unaccustomed to doing business the Japanese way.

This is an attempt to describe the various categories of groupings, see who belongs to some of the most important ones, and examine how they operate. It is impossible to tell everything in this or perhaps any book, for these groupings engage in exceptionally varied and extensive activities. Moreover, these units are sufficiently flexible and adaptable for their action to vary from case to case and over time. Finally, much of what they do is not generally disclosed to the public. Still, even a brief introduction can be of help.

In studying the groupings, especially if labeled with the increasingly unflattering name of *keiretsu*, it is essential to keep some balance. It would be unwise to ignore their activities or write them off as mere remnants of the past. It would be no less foolish to exaggerate the closeness of their links or their ability to throw up barriers to outsiders. This being said, a good look at these groupings is vital for any proper comprehension of Japanese business.

Just which combinations can be classified as *keiretsu* or groupings is sometimes difficult to determine since there are varying degrees of cooperation and considerable nuances in how they operate. It is generally agreed that there are six major *keiretsu* and perhaps a dozen other horizontal groupings of some importance. While there are large numbers of vertical groupings, since subcontracting is so widespread, there are only several dozen of particular note. As for the distribution *keiretsu*, they are even more limited because it has proven harder to structure (or restructure) marketing channels in the face of resistance from existing distributors.

While the number of groupings is small, several things must be remembered. First of all, each group can have many members. Some major *keiretsu* have accumulated a hundred or more. Just the 16 top horizontal and vertical groupings are estimated by a leading authority to have over a thousand members, and this only for those that are closely involved. And, of course, each one of these members may have its own subsidiaries and suppliers. Each vertical and distribution *keiretsu* can have dozens of members, even if usually of lesser size. This creates very extensive "families" of companies that can be related to one another.[1]

However, these are not just any companies. Those participating in the groups are often the largest and most prestigious. In fact, the ones that will be mentioned further on form almost a "who's who" of Japanese business. Among the horizontal groupings are names like Mitsubishi, Mitsui, Sumitomo, the Dai-Ichi Kangyo and Fuji Banks, and so on. Vertical groupings have been created by Hitachi, Matsushita and Sony, Toyota, Nissan and Honda, Nippon Steel, and more. Some of these also possess distribution *keiretsu*.

Beyond the name and prestige, it is essential to remember that the big companies in Japan also have great economic power. The 16 largest groups account for 26 percent of the total paid-up capital, 24 percent of annual sales, and 10 percent of the labor force.[2] A typology of the major groupings and the relations between them is provided in Figure 5.1.

Moreover, as groups, they are among the largest business entities in the world. The six banks that form the core of the big *keiretsu* are all among the top 20 internationally. Toyota and Nissan are the third and fourth ranking automobile companies, after General Motors and Ford, and are gaining on them. Hitachi and Matsushita are the sixth and seventh biggest electronics makers, but only for the moment. Other producers are in slightly less prominent positions in their sector, but most of them are gradually pulling ahead.

Finally, while such groupings do not prevail in all sectors, they are encountered in a fair number, including some of the most attractive. The horizontal *keiretsu* are deeply involved in services like banking, insurance, transport, and trading. They also engage in manufacturing. Vertical groupings are most noticeable in the automotive, electronics, steel, and shipbuilding industries. Distribution *keiretsu* exist for sales of automobiles, electronics, cosmetics, and pharmaceuticals. Even if less significant in other branches, the groupings do play some part in textiles and garments, household appliances, and even foodstuffs.

Considering the tremendous impact close relations can have on the way companies operate, it is essential to determine even roughly their effect on the Japanese economy. This has become a

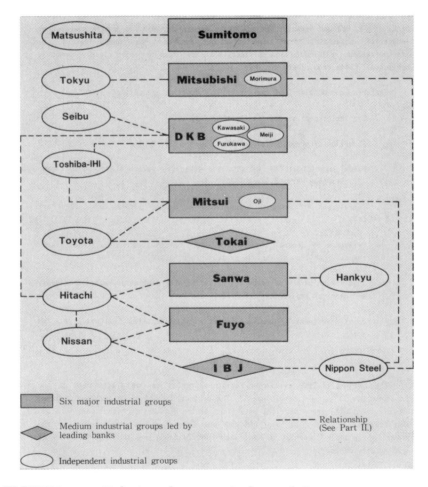

FIGURE 5.1. Relations between Industrial Groups
Credit: Dodwell Marketing Consultants, *Industrial Groupings In Japan,* 1984, p. 5.

controversial question in recent years. It was once admitted quite freely by Japanese officials and academics that the various *keiretsu* and groupings were not only numerous and influential but also a basic foundation of the economic structure. Since they have come under fire by Japan's trading partners as a possible barrier, their existence has been played down and occasionally almost denied by the authorities.[3]

But there can be little doubt as to their existence. What is more questionable is just how meaningful and effective the links are and, more pertinent, to what extent they influence behavior so as to restrict access to the market and distort economic forces. The reasons for uncertainty are many. After all, while such relations will move companies to do business together, even then they will work with outside firms if products are not available within the group or if outside suppliers offer better prices, quality, or service. The links thus encourage commercial transactions but do not guarantee them, and insiders benefit from certain advantages but not complete acceptance.

Moreover, while some companies are part of one grouping or another, many more are completely or largely independent. The *keiretsu* and groupings englobe only about 1 percent of all companies, leaving 99 percent to work by different rules. On the other hand, that 1 percent includes the largest and most dynamic companies, and they have a disproportionately large share of the nation's capital, sales, work force, and so on. Other firms tend to copy the groupings in at least some aspects since their influence on the business culture is so pervasive.

Thus, one can speak of the *keiretsu* as being typical and distinctive. But it is crucial that this be understood correctly and not be exaggerated. While there are certainly more such units in Japan, they are only one form of organization. Similar units and practices exist in other countries. The conglomerates are a case in point. Groups of this sort are more prevalent in some developing countries and parts of Western Europe than in the United States (though it was noticeable even in the United States in earlier years). The reasons why such groupings are less active abroad derive from differing historical, cultural, and social conditions, especially a more individualistic people and a more entrepreneurial business culture. But it can be traced as clearly to more effective antitrust legislation.

BONDS THAT HOLD

As indicated, these groupings assume quite different functions and can be subdivided into three categories: horizontal, vertical, and distribution *keiretsu*. Such a distinction is made for reasons of readier comprehension, since the activities vary considerably. But it should not be forgotten that all companies possess several functions, and thus one company may well fit into more than one category. It may, for example, be part of a banking alignment and also have its own integrated supplier network, or it may subcontract work and also control part of the distribution network.

Thus, the distinctions are described here largely to clarify their modus operandi. They should not cloud the fact that there are also many similarities between the groupings. In certain ways, they are just differing aspects or manifestations of the same underlying phenomenon. After all, some of the motives for such organization are rooted in ancient Japanese traditions, social customs, and mind-sets that affect many other features of the economy as well, most notably wholesale and retail distribution. Indeed, as soon as they are mentioned, it will be apparent that their impact is even broader and shapes, among other things, management techniques, labor relations, social institutions, and even politics.

An overriding concern for many Japanese businesses is loyalty and, related thereto, stability. It is therefore regarded as advantageous to create a more structured framework for business activities—for example, closer and steadier relations between manufacturers and suppliers or between manufacturers and distributors. This spawns the long-standing and time-honored relationships many Japanese take pride in. However, while less readily admitted, it also creates certain inefficiencies and restrictions that will be referred to later.

Of course, even in Japan it takes more than mere sentiment to forge solid and lasting ties. This has been noticed more by the locals than by most outside observers. The companies involved have created all sorts of links that bind them to one another in an equal-to-equal or superior-inferior relationship. It is impossible to comprehend the effectiveness (or at least solidity) and the workings of the companies concerned, without noting this aspect.

One link, the most visible, is through shareholding. In the horizontal groupings that bring together companies that are largely autonomous and roughly on an equal footing, this can take the form of cross-shareholding. Even then, there is a predominance of ownership emanating from certain core units such as banks, insurance firms, or trading companies. In the vertical groupings and distribution *keiretsu*, ownership is usually held by the parent company. The degree of ownership can range from majority to 100 percent, making the lesser body a mere affiliate or subsidiary; to less than 50 percent, giving the company reasonable leeway; to a few percent, which is little more than a token of interest.

Other connections are created by an exchange of personnel. Once again, this can be between loosely related companies on an equal footing, but it is far from prevalent in the case of vertical groupings and distribution *keiretsu*. Those transferred, seconded, or retired out to other firms, especially subsidiaries, can be at the top. This is done through the appointment of directors to related companies and, no less crucial, appointments of managers, auditors, or sales executives. At a lower level, this can consist of "lending" ordinary sales help to retail outlets. Given the importance of human relations in Japanese society, this subtler form of interpenetration can be extremely effective.

Some of the groupings are sufficiently structured and coordinated to have common bodies, such as the presidents' clubs of horizontal groupings. Others limit their contacts to periodic and sometimes quite informal meetings. But the vertical groupings and distribution *keiretsu*, given their ownership and direction, bring the subsidiaries (and also independent suppliers and outlets) into particularly tight units or exercise control in other ways. Another form of cooperation is for several bodies to launch joint ventures in which closer coordination than usual occurs, albeit for specific projects.

Financial connections are obviously important as well. Bank loans to group members and purchases of bonds by banks and insurance companies are just the most visible forms. This is done to encourage group members to deal not only with the lenders but also to deal with one another, since all are probably borrowers. Larger companies also help smaller ones financially. Trading companies lend to their suppliers and offer credit to their customers. Manufacturers guarantee loans for lesser suppliers and subcontractors who cannot provide adequate collateral.

The mere fact of doing business together for years has its influence. It is not only a question of knowing one another personally; suppliers have come to know the exact needs of their clients and cater to them most devotedly. They get considerable feedback without which no competitor would know what is desired. If the relationship is such that a large portion (perhaps all) of their sales is directed to one or several group members, they would think twice before leaving it. They would also think twice before dealing with a rival, even if for one article it offered better terms.

Finally, although it is hard to put one's finger on, there is a common ethos among the companies and their personnel. After all, they frequently sport the same badge and trademark and inspire a common image. Members keenly feel that they are part of a distinct group of companies, something that is essential in a society where employees relate so closely to their workplace and regard themselves more as company-men than free agents who can sell their skills anywhere. This encourages them to help one another and cooperate in various ways, many of which are hard to define but can have a significant impact.

This social and psychological element must always be borne in mind when one is tempted to write off the *keiretsu* due to a lack of mechanical ties. Some have claimed that *keiretsu* cannot be effective because, often enough, there is no centralized organization, or the crossholding is minor, or the companies have other sources of finance and clients. Wiser counsel comes from an expert on the subject, Dan Fenno Henderson: "The *keiretsu*, which is in organizational principle little more than a confederation, is uniquely effective in Japan because of the familial insider-outsider psychology and the efficacy of conciliar decision-making techniques. In Japan, these can mold an operable unit from such an unlikely organizational pattern."[4]

Similar causes naturally have similar effects. Companies that are members of groupings will work more closely together. Part of this is almost spontaneous since firms are closely related and their employees have a greater chance of knowing each other. Another part, probably the larger, results from design. The *keiretsu* and groupings were not created merely for social intercourse but for business purposes. They were carefully put together so that firms that complement one another's activities can cooperate to their mutual benefit.

The outcome has been a good deal of business flowing from one group member to another. In some cases, it is a relatively minor share of total sales that comes from other group members; in others, the level is significant. This is particularly true of the enterprise groupings, which generate much of the necessary supplies internally. It also aplies to a lesser extent to the distribution *keiretsu*, which sell a large share of the products. It is least significant among the horizontal *keiretsu*, which include members in a wide variety of fields, some of which have little to do with one another.

Statistics are hard to come by since many figures are not disclosed, especially as relates to transactions between subsidiaries and parent companies. The only ones given wide currency usually come from the Fair Trade Commission (FTC). Among other things, the FTC ascertained that members of the six top horizontal groupings cover about 20 percent of their financial needs from group institutions, and about 65 percent chose their lead bank from within the group.[5] Another FTC study traced the level of transactions between the six largest trading companies and their affiliates; the levels were 12 percent for purchases and 5 percent for sales.[6] While modest, these figures are far from negligible (and it must be recalled that the horizontal groupings are the loosest).

Given the commercial interaction with other members, the reverse obviously applies with regard to outsiders. There are fewer opportunities for unrelated firms to sell to members of horizontal groupings; there is even less room for them to supply parts to the vertical groupings; and they have trouble getting into that portion of the market that is dominated by distribution *keiretsu*. This aspect is less attractive and is therefore glossed over by those who participate in groupings and the government. If anything, they are at great pains to deny any exclusiveness. Still, if there is no advantage to being in a *keiretsu*, why bother?

NOTES

1. Dodwell Marketing Consultants, *Industrial Groupings in Japan*, Tokyo, 1984, pp. 40–49.

2. Ibid., pp. 40–41.

3. Fair Trade Commission, *The Fair Trade Commission's Approach to Trade Friction*, Tokyo, April, 1983.

4. Dan Fenno Henderson, *Foreign Enterprise in Japan*, Tuttle, Tokyo, 1975, p. 141.

5. See Fair Trade Commission, *The Present State of Industrial Groups*, Tokyo, June, 1983.

6. See Fair Trade Commission, *The Fair Trade Commission's Approach to Trade Friction*, Tokyo, April, 1983.

6
The Big Six . . .
And More

First, and in many ways foremost, of the various *keiretsu* are the horizontal groupings. Given the key position of the bank, they are also known as banking "alignments" or *kin'yu keiretsu*. They are the oldest groups—some tracing their origins back a century or more—and are the largest in terms of capital, sales, and employees. They also have the broadest scope since they include companies pursuing a wide range of activities. Finally, they possess the highest status and greatest political clout.

Three of these groups are extensions of the prewar *zaibatsu*, which were much tighter structures that were owned by wealthy families, controlled by holding companies, and run by managers with an interest in all aspects of their business. The *zaibatsu* played an even more decisive role in prewar economic development than the *keiretsu* since then. Some of this influence was negative, since the *zaibatsu* supported or tolerated the rise of militarism, colonial expansion, and then the war.

The occupation authorities moved to disband the *zaibatsu* as early as 1945. The families were dispossessed, numerous managers purged, groups split up, and even some individual companies divided. Some of the lesser *zaibatsu* disappeared. Mitsubishi, Mitsui, and Sumitomo, however, managed to survive, even if at first they were disjointed. Over the years they restored previous links, and in some cases companies merged back into their original form. After the revisions of the Antimonopoly Act in 1949 and 1953, they could shed any pretense of separateness and even operate under their old names.[1]

Several other groups—somewhat more loosely organized but quite similar in nature—arose through the efforts of influential banks to create their own groupings. These were banks with long histories that could attract old and new customers. They also absorbed parts of the lesser *zaibatsu* that had not reformed on their own. Those that have risen to true *keiretsu* status revolve around the Dia-Ichi Kangyo, Fuji, and Sanwa Banks. The groupings created by the Tokai Bank and Industrial Bank of Japan are weaker.

There are certain differences between the various horizontal groupings. For example, some are considerably larger than others. The biggest in every sense is Mitsubishi, with 144 member companies, almost 34 trillion yen in sales, and 360,000 employees. It is followed closely by Mitsui and Sumitomo, and a bit further off by the Fuji (or Fuyo), DKB, and Sanwa Groups. The Tokai and IBJ Groups are considerably smaller.[2]

A second difference arises with regard to the mix of companies. Some are more industrial, with Mitsubishi placing great stress on heavy industry and Sumitomo on metals. Others are more commercial, such as Mitsui. The bank-related groups tend to have less heavy and more light industry. Yet, with the huge number of members, each group displays impressive versatility, including most services, transport, industrial, financial, and real estate operations. Just how comprehensive and diversified a *keiretsu* can be is shown in Figure 6.1, giving the Mitsui Group as an example.

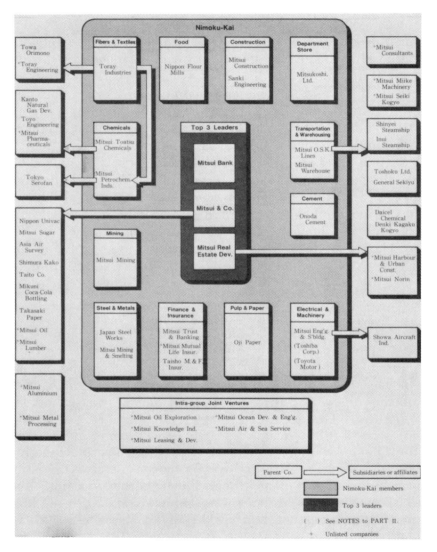

FIGURE 6.1.   The Mitsui Group

Credit: Dodwell Marketing Consultants, *Industrial Groupings in Japan,* 1984, p. 63.

More important than size in many ways is the degree of coordination. Here, too, the hierarchy runs pretty much along the same lines, with the older and larger units exercising stricter control. Each of these groups has an inner circle of members, about twenty or so, which can function more efficiently. They meet regularly (once a month) through presidents' councils. They discuss matters of common concern and are in a position to make important decisions. Just what the decisions are, and how far the solidarity reaches, is unknown since the proceedings are secret and rarely disclosed.

In addition to such meetings, there is a certain degree of crossholding, which usually takes the form of banks, insurance companies, and trading companies holding shares in industrial and other ventures. But some manufacturers hold shares in one another. Normally, each company has a rather small holding, a few percent or so, but several may join in and they can end up with 10 percent, 20 percent, or more between them. There are also cases where lesser members are practically the subsidiaries of major ones. The crossholding ratio varies from one group to the next, with a high of 21 percent in the Sumitomo Group and a low of 14 percent in the Sanwa Group.[3]

The links are further consolidated by appointing directors to one another's board. Again, it is more likely that the banks, insurance companies, and trading companies will send directors (and auditors) to the manufacturers, and manufacturers will send directors to companies they dominate. A study of the number of directors sent to group companies by key members showed as much as 5 percent of the total. To this can be added another 3 percent or so who came from government offices and public corporations. This government connection should not be ignored either.[4]

As will be noted periodically, while these relations are close, they are far from complete or exclusive. They are much weaker than the relations that existed among the prewar *zaibatsu*, and may be weakening even further. After all, members have relations with many companies that are outside the given grouping. Some adhere loosely to several groupings, and others have shifted from one to another over the years.

Moreover, these companies are all independent entities, albeit with some external control. They have their own boards of directors and managers, their own capital and employees, and they must fulfill their own corporate goals above all. If they were expected to do something that went against this principle, it is not certain they would comply. It is highly unlikely that such a thing would be asked of them by their peers—at least not without adequate compensation.

What is expected of the companies is not absolute dedication to the group's needs, but rather cooperation in their mutual interest and showing preference to their counterparts. This preference can be limited, occasionally even marginal, but it must be real in order to create the sort of solidarity that is necessary to maintain the group. From their continued existence and activities, it can be assumed that the members are willing to meet this relative commitment.

COOPERATION ECONOMY-WIDE

In each of these groups a decisive role is played by the bank, which is the primary source of finance for the group companies. This function was especially essential in the early period when the *keiretsu* were being formed. In order to reconstruct and expand, companies needed funds they could not generate internally or receive from the government. The importance of the bank has decreased somewhat since then as companies have increased their capitalization, expanded their internal funding, and can now raise money through stocks and bonds. But it has always been wise to remain on good terms with the bank.

The group bank was most often the lead bank of the other members. It was not their sole bank, but the one they turned to first and could be expected to give them privileged treatment. Most companies had another bank, occasionally several other banks, they could fall back on. But they borrowed more heavily from the group bank and thereby promoted its advancement. In return, it was easier for companies to get credit and it was also possible to do so on somewhat better interest and repayment terms.

Insurance companies play a subsidiary role in funding group members, often by purchasing their stock or bonds. In return, group members would give these companies priority when their services were needed. The shipping line would cover its risks, and the traders theirs, to the benefits of the marine insurers. Group members would give the fire, casualty, and life insurance companies priority in the same way. Again, they might also contract insurance elsewhere if the conditions were good enough, but that happened infrequently since they were favored customers.

Second only to the bank in its influence is the trading company or *sogo shosha*. Each group is tied up with one of those. The basic alignment is Mitsubishi with Mitsubishi Corp., Mitsui and Mitsui & Co., DKB with C. Itoh, Fuyo with Marubeni, Sumitomo with Sumitomo Corp., Sanwa with Nissho Iwai, and Tokai with Toyo Menka. Two of the smaller traders—Kanematsu-Gosho and Nichimen—have looser relations with DKB and Sanwa, respectively.

As is generally known, these nine *sogo shosha* play a dynamic role in Japan's trade. Their combined annual sales amounted to over 80 trillion yen in 1982, a figure that had been rising sharply until then but has since slowed down. Their ranking is as indicated above. The biggest, Mitsubishi, had a turnover of nearly 15 trillion yen, and even the smaller ones attained more than 3 trillion yen. These nine traders alone accounted for 48 percent of all exports and 56 percent of all imports.[5]

While the stress is often placed on their international activities, it should be noted that these companies actually import more than they export. They are also deeply involved in domestic distribution. In fact, domestic sales account for 40 percent of their total turnover, and their share of domestic wholesaling is close to 10 percent. The products they are most active in include petroleum and chemicals, steel and other metals, plant, machinery and construction, foodstuffs and textiles. In these sectors, and to a lesser extent elsewhere, it is hard not to encounter *sogo shosha* in one form or another.

Another function is financing. The *sogo shosha* regularly provide credit to the lesser companies they deal with. Domestically, this means giving local distributors or manufacturers advances or loans. While this makes these companies somewhat dependent on the trading company, it also works in the other direction in that the trading company must help them prosper if it is to earn a proper return on its money or, in bad times, avoid defaults. This is another reason why traders are partial to their own network.

Thus, while the *sogo shosha* are in the business of trading, they are not equally interested in dealing with every possible partner. They would tend not to cooperate with foreign companies that produce competitive goods. They prefer handling bulk commodities to processed ones since this is done locally by their clients. They would even tend not to take on finished products that compete directly with manufacturers whose exports they carry.

Manufacturers are an important part of this system. They often process the raw materials that are imported by the trading companies. As much as possible, they give priority to the *sogo shosha* in their own group. They also give it priority over foreign companies that might wish to sell them the same raw materials directly or in processed form. This precedence was particularly strict during the earlier period, but has since been relaxed somewhat. It has been realized that low-cost raw materials are essential, and more manufacturers are importing directly. Also, the cost of processing certain raw materials, such as bauxite for aluminum, is simply too high.

Manufacturers frequently cooperate with one another. The steel mills will sell much of their output to major users such as shipbuilders and automobile makers, some of which may well be in the group. They also pass it along to fabricators and smaller users. There is some amount of sales between more distant sectors, such as of chemicals to assorted manufacturers, paper to the whole range of firms, or computers to group offices across the board. Here, however, the relations become more tenuous and group membership is helpful but far from decisive.

While most of these transactions are current and ongoing, the groups also launch major projects that draw several of them into a joint company. Such companies have been set up, for example, for leasing, urban development, and information services. Others were mounted for overseas investments, especially in the mining and processing of raw materials.[6] This binds the partners closely together and makes it unlikely that they would seek outside sources.

While one should not exaggerate the effectiveness of these links, it is easy to see their advantages. They offer a foot in the door for any group member and a reasonable reception, something that is precious. They can perhaps clinch a sale even if the price, quality, or other conditions are not the very best but other dealings or group solidarity militate in favor. They may even urge their employees to purchase goods from related companies, as in Sumitomo's "buy Mazda" and "buy Asahi beer" campaigns.[7] When this happens, a company can count on a sales base that outsiders simply do not have.

What about outsiders? Where do they fit in? They are not actually excluded from doing business with group members. If they have a special item that is needed and not provided by anyone in the group, they would find ready entry. If they have a product that is not directly competitive, even if similar to those available, they may stand a chance. If their articles are directly competitive, things are more difficult. They can still sell, but they must fight for every sale and try to provide goods that are of even higher quality, at even lower prices, and with quite exceptional delivery and service.

NOTES

1. See William W. Lockwood, ed., *The State and Economic Enterprise in Japan*, Princeton University Press, Princeton, 1965, pp. 495–504.

2. For a description of the major *keiretsu*, see Dodwell, op. cit.

3. Dodwell, op. cit., p. 8. The crossholding ratio is defined as the shares held by group companies as a percentage of paid-up capital.

4. Ibid., pp. 11–2.

5. See Kunio Yoshihara, *Sogo Shosha*, Oxford University Press, Tokyo, 1982, and Alexander K. Young, *The Sogo Shosha: Japan's Multinational Trading Companies*, Westview, Boulder, 1979.

6. See Jon Woronoff, *Japan's Commercial Empire*, M. E. Sharpe, Armonk, 1984.

7. *Japan Economic Almanac 1985*, Japan Economic Journal, April, 1985, p. 216.

7

Industrial Groupings

While smaller and less diversified, the vertical groupings are exceedingly effective because they are aligned more strictly on a dominant enterprise, which explains why they are called enterprise (kigyo) keiretsu. They are characterized by far greater specialization and closer relations between the various members, which can be translated into enhanced commercial integration of their activities. They form much more of a self-contained unit and strive to be reasonably self-sufficient, an urge that affects the rest of the business community.

Just how many vertical groupings exist is a matter of conjecture; the number picked will depend mainly on the cutoff point. There are perhaps a dozen larger ones that have 30, 40, or more group members and boast a turnover of anywhere from 2 to 10 trillion yen. Their workforce reaches as high as 200,000 people. The top ones are, in order of membership size, Nippon Steel, Hitachi, Nissan, Toyota, Matsushita, Toshiba, Tokyu, and Seibu.[1] There are others that are not much smaller and many more that follow exactly the same pattern, although they cannot vie in size.

These groupings are vertical in the sense that they handle several links in the production chain. The Nippon Steel Group, for example, has members that are engaged in mining, general steel production, making of ordinary and special steels as well as other metals and ferroalloys, and finally manufacture of metallic products and machinery. Other members are less directly involved but contribute to the basic thrust, such as companies for construction, transportation, and trading.

Both Hitachi and Toshiba, makers of electronics and electrical equipment, cover this range with a series of generalized companies that produce a variety of products and more specialized ones for telecommunications, consumer articles, heating appliances, medical gear, or batteries. They extend into general machinery, transportation machinery, and plant engineering. This is rounded out with makers of wire and cable, chemicals, special steels, and tools.

The Matsushita Group is somewhat more focused on consumer electronics, although it has some companies making industrial items. Certain members produce parts while others turn out finished products like audio equipment, televisions and VCRs, refrigerators, or air conditioners. Nissan and Toyota produce a narrower range of finished products. But the variety of parts supplied by members is extensive: engines, transmissions, ventilators, carburetors, gaskets, springs, and on and on. This is the pattern not only for the companies mentioned but for just about all electronics and automotive companies. It is shown in some detail for the Matsushita Group in Figure 7.1

A looser, more varied structure exists for the groups that originally arose from private railway lines and spread in various directions, like Tokyu and Seibu. They have a land transportation unit, including the railway and perhaps bus lines, shipping, and aviation. Then comes real estate and construction due to their landholdings and need to build. But the emphasis has shifted into commerce, with trading and wholesale companies as well as department stores, supermarkets, and other retail outlets. Most recently, these groups added leisure services like recreation, hotels, and travel agencies.

The organization of these groupings, in which the pieces fit together so nicely, is much more constraining than in any of the horizontal groupings. That is primarily because the ownership position of the core or parent company is much stronger. Many of the group members are mere subsidiaries, and in those that enjoy some autonomy the shareholdings are much higher, often 50 percent or more.

This development has come about in three ways. Some companies spin off new firms as their divisions expanded, the path taken largely by Hitachi and Toyota. Others absorbed or bought into going concerns that ran into trouble or needed financial and management assistance. This was more the case for Nissan, although that sort of thing happens throughout the groupings. The third technique was to establish joint ventures with other group members, nongroup members, or foreign companies. In

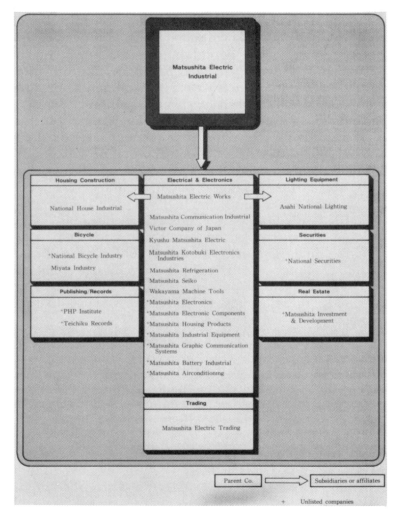

FIGURE 7.1.   The Matsushita Group

Credit: Dodwell Marketing Consultants, *Industrial Groupings in Japan*, 1984, p. 133.

addition to actual group members, there are slews of suppliers and subcontractors who provide mainly parts or services.

The units assimilated in these ways are not only small companies but full-fledged groups (and sometimes erstwhile rivals) like Fuji Heavy Industries for Nissan, Hino and Diahatsu for Toyota, and Victor Company of Japan for Matsushita. More impressive is the interlinking of Toshiba and Ishikawajima-Harima Heavy Industries (IHI), itself a leading shipbuilder and maker of machinery and metal products. This was arranged through a crossholding of shares, with Toshiba becoming the major shareholder of IHI.

Naturally, a commanding ownership position was used to exert substantial control over the group members. This could be done through the appointment of directors (and even presidents) and transfer of personnel. It also took the form of presidential councils or more informal clubs of company executives, always under the chairmanship of the group leader. Even stricter in the imposition of rules were the associations created for the suppliers and subcontractors, working them into the production scheme of the assembler.

Nor should it be forgotten that some of these groups are not the bureaucratic units that are supposedly typical of Japan, but groups that were formed by dynamic entrepreneurs and where the founder or his heirs are still acitve, such as Matsushita, Toyota, Tokyu, and Seibu. There—no matter what the organigrams may show—leadership emanates from one man and his close associates, and there are limited possibilities of evading this further down.

The last factor is commercial. Most of the group members are the suppliers or clients of one another and constantly do business together. In this relationship, it tends to be the client that has the upper hand. The client can impose its will all the more readily to the extent that it is the biggest, and in many cases the sole, buyer. The regulation is most stringent as regards the suppliers' networks in which parts are procured by automotive or electronics makers. It is somewhat less effective where makers of finished goods can offer their products to a broader range of clients. If they have to sell through the trading, wholesale, or retail firms run by the parent company, there is additional pressure.

That this is not theoretical, and that the leverage is very real, can be shown from several examples that are quite close to the norm. Fuji Tekko, a maker of transmission and axle parts, is owned to 34 percent by Nissan and sells 86 percent of its output to Nissan. Nippondenso, an electrical parts maker, is owned to 22 percent by Toyota(and another 7 percent by Toyoda Loom) and sells 58 percent of its output to Toyota.[2] Even Fuji Heavy Industries, of which Nissan is a shareholder, makes Nissan cars along with its own Subaru. Both Hino and Daihatsu produce large numbers of Toyotas. Many members of the Matsushita family, even though relatively autonomous on paper, still sell through Matsushita Electric Trading and thousands of local shops.[3]

As must be evident, each one of these vertical groupings is a large and powerful unit in its own right. But most of them are also part of, or at least related to, one of the major horizontal groupings. The relations can take some of the forms referred to earlier. The primary relations are financing from the banks and trading through the *sogo shosha*. Thus, Nissan is part of the Fuyo Group and Toyota sits on both the Mitsui and Tokai Group council, borrowing largely from those banks. Hitachi is somewhat more independent, dealing with the Fuji, Sanwa, and DKB banks and sitting on the council of the first two. Nippon Steel sells through Mitsui & Co. and Mitsubishi Corp., as both groups lack a large steel manufacturer.

This linkage enhances the position of both units, horizontal and vertical. It increases the concentration of productive and marketing capabilities and ties even more companies into a broader nexus whose ramifications cannot possibly be overlooked.

KEEPING IT ALL IN THE "FAMILY"

From even the briefest description of this system it is reasonably clear how it works. It is essentially an institutionalization of the subcontracting networks that exist everywhere, but are usually rather fluid and informal. This time the units are worked into a hierarchical structure from which the dominant or parent companies procure their necessary parts, materials, and services. This makes for an extremely integrated production machine, which is doubtlessly one of the secrets of Japan's industrial success.

The process is easiest to grasp in the automotive industry. There, the automakers are just assemblers who produce relatively few parts on their own. The bulk of the parts come from a number of primary suppliers that produce engines, electrical parts, drive, transmission, and steering parts, suspension and brake parts, body parts, and accessories. Other companies provide the metal, rubber, glass, plastic, and other basic materials. Both of these sets of suppliers may well be group members, especially the former. How this is done in the Nissan Group is shown in Figure 7.2

Beneath this are further layers of secondary, tertiary, and lesser subcontractors. Some produce items that go into the parts like springs, screws, forgings, castings, and pressings. Others engage in necessary activities such as plating, painting, welding, and so on. These are usually very small firms, perhaps partly owned by the group members or suppliers—if not, certainly dependent on them.

It is hard to exaggerate how complete this supplier network is since, for all practical purposes, it is capable of suppying just about every part, material, or service the assembler could possibly use. Should there be a gap somewhere, it would not be surprising if the parent company were to set up a new subsidiary. It is impossible to tell what share of the total value of a finished automobile, say, is generated from among group members or subsidiaries, but it is certainly the overwhelming majority.

The other vertical groupings also operate on the same basis to meet their specific needs. The electrical and electronics companies have parts suppliers, many of them captive, a fair number actually group members. The steel and shipbuilding companies are also well endowed with suppliers and, often more important, subcontractors. They will handle such tasks as welding and painting in addition to supplying certain parts.

There is a second advantage to these groups that is particularly adapted to Japanese needs. In a business community where it is common to develop deep and lasting relations, it would be unpleasant if an established client were not able to obtain what it wanted from a traditional supplier. The client might

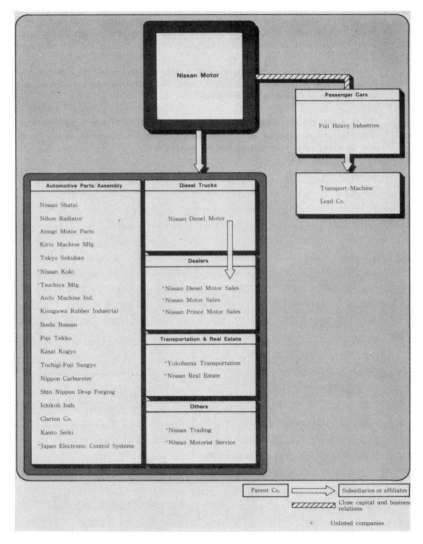

FIGURE 7.2.   The Nissan Group

Credit: Dodwell Marketing Consultants, *Industrial Groupings in Japan*, 1984, p. 124.

then be forced to go shopping elsewhere, which would be awkward. It would be considerably more disagreeable for the supplier, since it is conceivable that the client might stray. Having purchased one article, the client might notice others and be drawn into a close relationship with a competitor.

Japanese manufacturers, and especially groups, therefore tend to produce just about everything they can in their own line. They want to have the broadest possible range so that there is no need to turn to anyone else. This applies most aptly to the electrical and electronics and automotive industries, but it applies to others as well, such as producers of textiles, chemicals, and pharmaceuticals and even publishers.

This could take the form, for example, of major automobile makers like Toyota and Nissan producing cars of varied size and style to cover much of the market. The gaps are then filled through associates like Daihatsu and Fuji. But it is more pronounced for electrical goods, especially household appliances and consumer electronics. Each one of the top makers produces just about every possible article so that someone entering its store will not have to look elsewhere.

Once again, should there be some gap, the inclination is to fill it from within the group. It would, of course, be feasible to import the item and this is sometimes done, at least in the initial period. But few articles are so special that they could not be produced by one member or another of the extensive company "family." This is not difficult for a firm like Toyota, say, with 220 primary suppliers and over a thousand secondary and tertiary ones, or Matsushita with over 500 subsidiaries and affiliates.[4]

The integration of the railway-retailing empires like Tokyu and Seibu displays some of these aspects, but in a much less acute form since they are in fields that are not as directly related. True, the travel agency, located in the department store, can sell tickets on the airline or weekends in the hotel. Customers can be encouraged to buy insurance or use credit. And the railway line is a major conveyance to the department store. But this does not add up to much.

Similarly, there has been some diversification so that a customer can stick to the company. Thus, alongside the original railway line, there are now bus and other transport companies, shipping firms, and airlines. More striking is the knack of these groups, and most major retailers, to assume different forms to get into different market segments and price categories. Both Tokyu and Seibu have not only department stores but supermarkets (known as superstores), convenience or specialty stores, and fast food outlets. This has been done by most of the major retailers, including Daiei, Ito-Yokado, Jusco, and so on.[5]

There is no question about the advantages of the system to the parent company. It is guaranteed, more than could possibly be obtained from independent suppliers, on-time delivery, good quality, and low price. It can make its production plans and sales forecasts known to the suppliers, which can then adjust their own schedules accordingly. Due to the close relations, if it is necessary to introduce a new product, the design and other particulars can be worked out together. If, for any reasons, the parent company were in financial difficulty, it could prevail on its suppliers to bear some of the brunt and decrease their prices.

There are also advantages for the suppliers. They can count on a steady stream of orders and will find it easier to plan their future operations. If in difficulty, they may get financial and management assistance. Admittedly, in such a tight situation, it is hard for them to make very big margins, but this would seem to be compensated for by the stability of the relationship. While they may have to compress prices when things are rough, they may be able to get a bit more in boom times. Or, if pressed hard, they can exert some pressure on their own subcontractors.

There is a definite mood of "all in the same boat" in these arrangements. Some of it comes from the human connections, since subsidiaries often have directors who have been appointed to them and other personnel who may have retired there. They will naturally maintain their allegiance to the parent company, but also look out for their new colleagues. Some also comes from the financial connections. As a shareholder, often a major one, it would be foolish to hurt profits that one subsequently receives as dividends.

Where does this leave outsiders? In a disadvantageous position, to say the least. It is difficult to make sales because the whole system is so closely integrated and there are almost no gaps. Just about anything a parent company, assembler, or retailer might want can be made by another company it is related to in one way or another. Only in very special cases—where an

exceptional new product is launched or the producer has proprietary rights—is it necessary to turn to an outsider.

NOTES

1. For a description of the major vertical groupings, see Dodwell,
op. cit.

2. See Dodwell, *The Structure of the Japanese Auto Parts Industry*,
Tokyo, 1983.

3. See Dodwell, *Key Players in the Japanese Electronics Industry*,
Tokyo, 1985.

4. Ibid.

5. See Dodwell, *The Structure of the Japanese Retail and Distribution Industry*, Tokyo, 1985.

8

From Manufacturing To Marketing

The third category of groupings is less known but no less effective for that. It is the distribution *keiretsu (ryutsu keiretsuka)*,
also translated as "distribution channeling arrangements" and
"integrated marketing networks." Smaller, less capitalized, and
less visible, they have the tremendous advantage of being closest
to the final consumer. That is where their real power comes from
and why anyone doing business with Japan would be most unwise to dismiss them.

The distribution *keiretsu* strictly speaking consist of groupings in which the manufacturer controls or dominates the

marketing channels for its products, often down to the last detail. It may set up its own wholesale operations and sell to other secondary or tertiary wholesalers. Or it may reach further to the retail outlets, which it sometimes owns, sometimes merely manipulates.[1]

The derivation of these groupings is partly historical. Some sectors were new to Japan when they arose in prewar days or were resumed after the war, and there were not enough wholesalers or retailers to handle them. In order to sell the goods, the makers had no choice but to create their own marketing machinery, their own wholesaling operations, and sometimes even the local dealerships or neighborhood stores that carried the goods. This occurred for household appliances, sewing machines, consumer electronics, automobiles, motorcycles, and Western musical instruments.

In other sectors, it was the importer that branched into production. Realizing that the goods could be produced as well, as cheaply, and more conveniently in Japan—while giving the entrepreneur a healthy value added—wholesalers either set up their own companies or entrusted related companies with the task. In some cases, these were joint ventures with foreign companies that possessed the know-how. This path was taken most notably in sporting goods and pharmaceuticals, with production quickly overtaking marketing as the pivot.

The other reasons were similar to those that moved businesses to create groupings in all other sectors, such as loyalty and stability of the relationship. By controlling the outlets, it was easier to be certain that sales would be undertaken actively and that the wholesaler or retailer would not readily switch to another maker. For this, it was necessary to make the marketing channels do the producer's bidding rather than the other way around.

Control was imposed by means that should be familiar by now. The producer held shares in the wholesaler, when it was not a wholly-owned venture, and sometimes also in the retailers, although less frequently and less extensively. For historical reasons, it might also occur that the wholesaler held stock in the producer. This shareholding enabled the lead company to impose directors on the sales outlets and, in some instances even more important, to have someone sitting in the committees that decided just which products to carry and how hard to push them.

Although not at quite as high a level, there was a further practice whose benefits can hardly be overlooked. Manufacturers would occasionally "lend" their personnel to the retailers. These were usually junior employees who thereby gained contact with the public and learned about the trade. More important, of course, was that they appeared wearing the company uniform or badge and encouraged customers to buy company products. This was often done with even more zeal than by the proprietor of the outlet who, not wishing to upset the supplier and habitually short-staffed, went along with the exercise.

In other cases, where there was no actual ownership, wholesale outlets might become financially dependent on the manufacturer due to the need for credit.[2] The situation of most retailers was even more delicate since they always had a skimpy cash flow and easily became dependent on rebates. Providing credit was not only a necessary task; it was done specifically to create such a state of dependence, which permitted the manufacturers or wholesalers to impose their will on the retailers.

As mentioned, this sort of relationship arose especially in certain sectors, including automobiles and motorcycles, household appliances and consumer electronics, optical goods (eyeglasses, cameras), pharmaceuticals, cosmetics, sewing machines, and alcoholic beverages. It also emerged for musical instruments, sporting goods, and even foodstuffs. Companies that use the technique extensively include such well-known names as Matsushita (and most other electronics makers), Nissan, Toyota (and their rivals), Shiseido (and other cosmetics firms), Suntory (and other brewers and distillers), K. Hattori (for Seiko watches), Nippon Gakki (electones, pianos, and other instruments), and Hoya (eyeglasses).

However, makers of other articles that are not normally sold directly to the final consumer were forced to do so by another quirk of the distribution system. Department stores, and even supermarkets to some extent, rent out stalls or floor space to manufacturers, which are expected to decorate, staff, and supply them with goods. Makers therefore have to go into marketing even if the overall establishment is not theirs. Articles frequently sold this way include cosmetics and fashion goods, household furnishings and furniture, and foreign and domestic foods.

While they are not truly distribution *keiretsu*, there are other arrangements that sometimes use similar techniques and end up with roughly the same results. These are relationships in which it is the marketing unit that controls the producers. Since that unit may be not just one or two distributors but a whole family of retailers, it can be exceedingly effective. A good example of this are the Tokyu and Seibu Retail Groups. This composition of the latter is given in Figure 8.1.

Another variation occurs with the *sogo shosha*. Their main activity is to import commodities and raw materials in bulk. But they do not always sell them directly. In order to simplify their task and acquire the necessary expertise, they tend to create separate wholesalers for different product lines. Some of those working with the big nine deal in special steels and other metals, petroleum and gas, chemicals, textiles, plant and equipment, or foodstuffs.

The trading companies also go a big step further by setting up or joining with other firms that process their bulk imports. Just a few among the many ventures undertaken by the nine top traders include making of steel sheet, wire, pipe, etc., plastic products, timber, fertilizer, and so on. They are most active in foodstuffs. Such units produce edible oils, frozen fish and meat, soft drinks, and refined sugar.

Wholesalers, whether independent or integrated into the general trading companies, also engage in such production activities. As noted, the pharmaceutical wholesalers were so ambitious that they eventually turned into manufacturers. Others have done the same for their own product lines, whether chemicals, foodstuffs, sporting goods, or toys.

Finally, and most recently, the major department and chain stores have taken to selling more products under their own brand. This is being done by Tokyu and Seibu, and even more aggressively by Daiei and Ito-Yokado. Smaller chains are also joining in. The articles include especially clothing, household goods, and foodstuffs. Private brand sales already amount to about a tenth of total turnover. At first products were made by existing manufacturers, but the retailers have been increasingly setting up their own operations.

In these setups, the shareholding is much higher than it is for horizontal groupings or distribution *keiretsu*. Most are well over 50 percent, and 100 percent ownership seems to be the goal, one that is frequently attained. From such a position it is easy to exercise control as regards not only appointment of directors but also

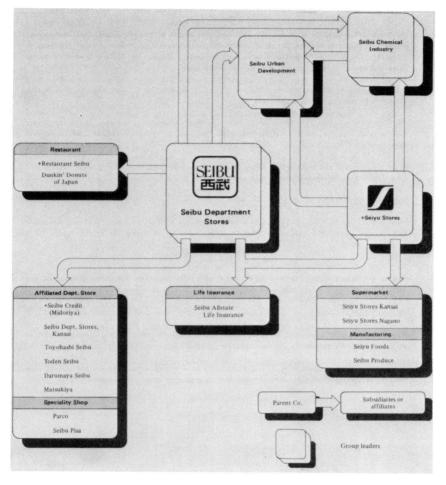

FIGURE 8.1. The Seibu Retail Group

Credit: Dodwell Marketing Consultants, *The Structure of the Japanese Retail and Distribution Industry,* 1981, p. 83.

the whole staff. This influence penetrates all aspects of the subsidiaries' activities.

Whatever the type of arrangement, the relationship between manufacturers and distributors is uncommonly close in Japan. Indeed, as pointed out by Mark Zimmerman, a long-time businessman and former president of the American Chamber of Commerce in Japan, the distribution network is actually "an extension of the company itself." As he indicates: "Senior executives are obligated to visit each distributor at least once a year to reaffirm their commitment. Similarly, the distributor will visit the head office, rest houses, factories, and branches of the Japanese company, knowing that he will be treated like an honored family member."[3]

The other side of this close relationship is that little room remains for newcomers, local or foreign. As Zimmerman notes: "The existing distribution network is restricted to current manufacturers, and it is unlikely to be susceptible to an offer to switch to a new, untried manufacturer. Building a distribution network from scratch can take many years, which is one of the main reasons why foreign companies have trouble expanding in Japan unless they can piggyback on the already existing network of a joint-venture partner."[4]

DOMINATING DISTRIBUTION

The motives for establishing these groupings have already been described by echoing the standard Japanese allusions to stability and loyalty. These are, indeed, fine virtues. But they can be more than that. They can be excellent commercial principles that redound to the credit of the dominant party. It only takes some simple illustrations to show this.

Loyalty means, among other things, that the wholesalers and retailers will continue selling the manufacturer's goods year after year. It also implies that, as part of the "family," they will do their best to sell effectively. They will cultivate the clientele, look after its needs, and provide efficient service. They will probaby throw themselves even more wholeheartedly into the exercise if, as is the underlying aim, they accept exclusivity. Most of the wholesalers and retailers concerned are either bound by contract as sole agents or simply tend to sell only one maker's products for financial or sentimental reasons.

This also makes it easier to accomplish some subsidiary aims of the manufacturer. For example, it is possible for the manufacturer to create a uniform image by imposing its publicity, POS gadgets, mottoes and slogans, and even shop and shelf layout. It can also obtain better feedback since the retailers are more likely to indicate which products do well or poorly, how they can be improved to satisfy the customers, what articles are missing, and so on. The feedback could hardly be more direct than when it passes through sales help loaned to the retailer.

There is a final element, one that is not as noble but certainly plays a crucial role: price. By controlling much of the wholesale and retail network, it is possible to impose fixed prices at which the goods must be sold. Under most contracts, retailers cannot pass goods along to third parties, which might then lower the price, nor would they find it wise to discount goods themselves if warned not to. Resale-price maintenance helps the manufacturer most as it boosts profits. That it may reduce sales is a problem for the retailer.[5]

These are more than ample causes for manufacturers to set up or preserve their own marketing channels. It would seem that the motives of the trading companies, wholesalers, or retailers that establish production operations would be considerably different. In one way they are, in that they seek advantages similar to those of vertical groupings, which want reliable flows of quality products at cheap prices. If they cannot obtain this, they would have been just as well off using established companies.

But as the major or sole owner of manufacturers, they cannot help working in the latters' interest as well. They must make every effort to sell the goods or their subsidiaries will be stuck with excess stock or capacity. They must see that the margins are reasonable or they cannot pay personnel and other costs and still have a profit, part of which they collect. They can hardly escape noting that when they sell their own brand goods, as opposed to those of outside suppliers, they not only earn a commission but dividends as well.

One essential dimension of these groupings has been neglected; until it is adequately fathomed, much of the discussion is meaningless. For if the manufacturers had only modest numbers of outlets amidst vast numbers of retailers or dealers who sold the products of several makers—or, quite simply, any maker that offered a proper commisssion—this phenomenon could be regarded as secondary. That the situation is the complete opposite elevates it to exceptional prominence.

In those sectors where distribution *keiretsu* appear, the vast majority of the outlets might be tied up with one maker or another. This happens for automobiles, motorcycles, cosmetics, eyeglasses, watches, household appliances, consumer electronics, and other articles. In these sectors, it is the exception to encounter a choice of brands. When that exists, the choice may only be in appearance with the others just filling out the range of the principal maker with items that are much cheaper, more expensive, or somehow different.

To get an idea of the dimensions involved, it might be pointed out that about five thousand electronics retail outlets belong to the *keiretsu* of Matsushita, Toshiba, Hitachi, Mitsubishi, Sanyo, Sharp, and Sony. Only two thousand are independent. For automobiles the situation is even more extreme: Toyota has over 4,200 sales units, Nissan and the others proportionately less. Hardly anybody sells competing imported cars. The same thing happens for motorcycles, where Honda, Yamaha, and Suzuki control most of the outlets, or for eyeglasses with Hoya and watches with Seiko.

Given the role of small retail outlets and the tendency of many Japanese to shop locally, it is decisive for a manufacturer to have an extensive and dense network. If it is not in a given neighborhood, it is entirely possible that it will not sell goods there. Indeed, there is even a close correlation between the number of outlets and market share. Using the electronics industry as an example, Matsushita is the top producer with Sony much further down, doubtlessly a function of their marketing machinery in part.

For the third time, it is necessary to consider the position of the outsider. Here, the disadvantages can be even more telling since, if it cannot reach the end consumer, it is hard to sell no matter how good, cheap, or desirable the products.

The first stumbling block arises with the trading companies and the wholesalers, which are widely regarded as the principal gateways to the Japanese market. If one of these companies produces competing goods or has close relations with a manufacturer that does, it is naturally less interested in taking up the goods of outsiders. The situation is still more congenial with chain stores, since their own production is rather limited. But, in all cases, it is most likely that they will gradually be filling their own needs where those needs are largest and most regular, leaving only lesser niches open.

The chances for entry are even more restricted with the distribution *keiretsu*. They were designed specifically to sell the manufacturer's goods and not those of its competitors. Retailers that have been lined up would not break this compact unless there were very tempting advantages. Given the large number of captive outlets, the remainder offer only limited access to the market. The rising discount houses or the shops in Akihabara are an alternative, but it will take some time for them to shift the balance.

NOTES

1. See Dodwell, *The Structure of the Japanese Retail and Distribution Industry*, Tokyo, 1985.

2. Mark Zimmerman, *How to do Business with the Japanese*, Random House, New York, 1985, p. 137.

3. Ibid., p. 138.

4. Ibid., p. 139.

5. See J. Amanda Covey, "Vertical Restraints under Japanese Law," *Law in Japan*, Vol. 14, 1981, pp. 49–81, and Hideto Ishida, "Anticompetitive Practices in the Distribution of Goods and Services in Japan: The Problems of the Distribution Keiretsu," *Journal of Japanese Studies*, Vol. 9, No. 2, Summer 1983, pp. 319–34.

9

Beating The System

No matter how much the Japanese government protests that its market is open and businesses deny that their arrangements obstruct trade, it is obvious that the existence of numerous groupings is a barrier of sorts.[1] Even when it is not an absolute barrier, it creates restraints or constricts the room for maneuver. This is done not only for a few products but for a broad spectrum: from raw materials and capital goods to manufactures and quite ordinary consumer articles. It can happen at the level of trading companies and wholesalers, manufacturers or distributors.

This, of course, makes Japan a more difficult market, but it does not make it a completely closed market. Many foreign companies do operate here and foreign goods are regularly bought and sold. What is necessary is to recognize the existence of these groupings and learn how to live with them. As long as the system is what it is, there is little point in businesses lamenting the difficulties as opposed to figuring out how to work with, or around, these groupings and beat the system.

This can be done in various ways. In fact, when describing how foreign companies have succeeded, it immediately becomes obvious just how important these groupings are. This special playing field also explains the standard "solutions" proposed by the primers and consulting firms that advise foreigners on how to do business in Japan.

The presentation of these various ways and means, in addition to indicating the principal channels, will trace another sort of progression: from a lesser to a greater degree of effort on the part of the exporter or manufacturer. This can demonstrate in a sense the extent of the foreign company's commitment to the Japanese market.

The starting point for those selling bulk commodities and raw materials is usually the trading companies and not, as in many other places, the actual users. The *sogo shosha* purchase in vast quantities and then distribute, directly or through wholesalers, to the users. It would be hard to break into these channels, and that fact has largely been accepted. Thus, each year millions of tons of coal, iron, and other mineral ores, oil, gas, wheat, and other foodstuffs pass through the larger traders and sometimes through more specialized houses.

Capital goods are also channeled primarily through trading companies. They may, on occasion, be bought directly by the user, but more often they pass through the traders. Here, the role of the smaller companies is more highly appreciated, with units that specialize in machine tools, metalworking equipment, woodworking equipment, and so on. Most foreign producers concede this and find it far easier than trying to sell alone.

Producers of parts and components often have more difficulty in finding a channel, given the vertical *keiretsu*. The major assemblers and makers do not deal much with the trading companies and tend to procure everything locally. They may occasionally buy something from foreign sources, but the more likely route is through a foreign supplier that has tied up with one of their own subsidiaries. Only when pushed to do so by government action—as when urged on by the U.S. Congress, for example—have token purchases been forthcoming.

There is much more scope for producers of equipment that may be purchased by many smaller companies or, even more so, consumer goods, since the market is more dispersed and individual choice plays a greater role. This applies to larger items like earth-moving equipment, machinery, or elevators. It also includes automobiles, audio and video equipment, cameras and optical goods, furniture and household furnishings, clothing, food, and so on. For these products, and many more, there is not only one channel but sometimes a profusion of channels, and it is essential to pick the right one.[2]

In choosing the channel, it is necessary for the exporter to make two crucial decisions. First of all, does it want to use a general trading company or a specialized house? Both have advantages and drawbacks. The *sogo shosha* have a broader sweep, bigger network, and so on. But they tend to take on only very large quantities of goods and not to be overly interested in smaller runs or lesser products. This, to the contrary, is of more interest to specialized traders.

The other question, however, cuts in the opposite direction. Does the channel handle competing products that may make it reject the foreign exporter or give its products second-rate treatment? Such an occurrence is somewhat less likely for the general than the specialized traders, since the latter by their nature have to provide everything in the specific line. In addition, they are more likely either to own their own production subsidiaries or be dominated by local manufacturers.

The choice is not easy. A specialized firm or a *sogo shosha* with considerable experience in the sector will have a larger and stronger marketing network. But that is of little avail if it cannot be used fully. Still, in the end, most foreign makers accept the fact that they may not get the best care and stick to an experienced distributor. Others go out of their way to seek a trader or importer that does not carry exactly the product they have and therefore fills a niche.

Companies that used the *sogo shosha* as a point of entry are too numerous to mention and come from every conceivable branch. Specialized traders have been particularly popular in certain sectors, including machinery of all sorts where expertise and after-sale service are essential. Specialized traders and importers have also been very active for alcoholic beverages, confectionaries, and special foods. Some of these traders are foreign firms like Caldbeck-MacGregor, Jardine, and Dodwell. Automobiles have been distributed almost exclusively by specialized importers, Yanase being the largest.

But some exporters have gone completely out of the sector, dealing with a company known to be a good distributor even if not for the same product. The best known example here is Warner Lambert, which went into a tie-up with K. Hattori to sell Schick razors. Hattori used the same distribution network, although somewhat different channels, as it had developed for sales of Seiko watches. This proved to be a resounding success. Volvo, after using a specialized automobile importer for some years, switched to Teijin, a textile company. Here, too, it was able to boost sales, if not as strikingly.[3]

Another way of getting into the market by leaving most of the burden to a domestic company is through licensing. The

Japanese manufacturer, in exchange for a royalty, produces and sells the goods locally. The advantages are, in every case, to be closer to the users or consumers, improve feedback, and provide after-sale service. Advantages may also include, if the local manufacturer is well chosen, enhanced quality and lower prices due to cheaper transport costs and perhaps greater efficiency. This route has been taken so often that there is no point in referring to specific cases—they number in the tens of thousands.

More complex than either working passively through Japanese distribution channels or licensing production is the establishment of a joint venture.[4] This can handle either one of the aforementioned tasks or, in many cases, both. Some joint ventures are set up to have better contact with the distributors. By skipping the trading company or importer and going directly to local wholesalers, it is possible to develop a better sense of the market. By creating one's own sales force in addition, marketing can be refined and the sales effort intensified. It is also possible to provide direct input into advertising campaigns.

The other side of the joint venture may be to manufacture locally while getting more involved in the process. It is not just a question of providing know-how and letting another company take over. The originator of the product, especially if it enjoys proprietary rights, can see that operations are in keeping with its desiderata. It can also benefit from any refinements in the production techniques or products rather than these going to the Japanese firms alone. The originator may also get the hang of manufacturing in Japan, which can be useful.

Some joint ventures were organized essentially to benefit from existing distribution networks.[5] This applies to all of the pharmaceutical joint ventures arranged with wholesalers, such as the links between Bayer or Searle and Yakuhin, Lederle and Takeda, and Smith Kline and Fujisawa. It also applies to foodstuffs, such as Meiji-Borden, Ajinomoto-General Foods, and Kirin-Seagram. Finally, many of the high fashion brand-name goods are really the fruit of joint ventures. Although not the primary cause, for reasons of convenience, cost, perishability, or bureaucratic regulations, much of the manufacturing is done locally as well.

Joint ventures established basically to engage in manufacturing, although also with an eye to distribution, are somewhat less numerous. One reason is the tremendous capital costs involved. However, while high, it is certainly cheaper to do this with a local partner than go it alone, which explains why there are so many. Prominent among them are Caterpillar-Mitsubishi, Du Pont-Toray, and Nissan's production of the Volkswagen Santana.

There is a third form of joint venture that is becoming increasingly popular. It involves franchising. But the unusual twist is that most often the foreign franchiser does not recruit its franchisees directly; it ties up with a major Japanese company that then, on its own or through a joint venture, builds up the network. This has been done by Kentucky Fried Chicken with Mitsubishi and by McDonald's with Fujita. In another variation, Japanese chain stores have united with their foreign counterparts to set up convenience stores, such as Seibu with Family Mart and Ito-Yokado with Seven-Eleven. Finally, although even more different, it should be mentioned that while Coca-Cola (Japan) produces the renowned beverage, bottling and distribution are done through tie-ups with leading firms like Mitsui, Mitsubishi, Kirin, and so on.[6]

It is a much bigger step to move from this level to the wholly-owned operation. Not only are there increased costs for renting premises, hiring personnel, and making one's presence known, but also the tasks that will be handled are themselves intrinsically expensive. The two primary ones are again distribution and production.

Some foreign companies set up shop mainly for distribution purposes. Instead of selling to a trading company or importer, they wanted to piece together their own network of wholesalers. That this is not simple is shown by the fact that one of the most successful, Johnson & Johnson, deals with hundreds of different ones. Even more remarkable was Nestlé's ability to manipulate old and new routes to sell Nescafé, Brite, Milo, and other products.[7] Other companies have taken the easy way out, purchasing the wholesaler they worked with, as Proctor & Gamble for one line. In order to have a solid distribution organization, some pharmaceutical companies have absorbed their former partners.

Even more difficult is to create one's own outlets or recruit a team of door-to-door sales personnel. The latter was done with particular verve by some of the cosmetics firms, especially Revlon and Max Factor. It is also being done by Electrolux for its vacuum cleaners and other products. A more ambitious operation was launched recently by BMW: it left its former importer-agent to create its own string of dealerships.

In these sectors, distribution was the main concern. However, there is a trend to have products manufactured locally as well, especially for cosmetics, fashions, foods, and smaller consumer articles. This can be done by local companies with no real difficulty. It is much more challenging to open one's own factory, and this may become necessary in order to control the process, protect proprietary rights, or become fully accepted in the marketplace. This has been done most impressively by IBM, which is one of the oldest foreign companies and holds the top position for sales. Other computer or semiconductor makers have gone over to local manufacture as well.

The above proves that it is possible to do business in Japan. It also proves that the impediments are real, for not all companies can use the existing and somewhat constricted channels. The traders, and even the wholesalers to some extent, are interested in handling only relatively large quantities of goods, and give preference to those that have some special value. The Japanese license only sophisticated technologies and, as their own level rises, fewer firms can provide them. There are also fewer candidates for joint ventures since Japanese companies can produce much of what they want. Finally, the capital costs of creating a distribution network or opening a production facility are enormous.

This means that those who can benefit from the possible "solutions" are rather limited. They are usually the biggest, most technologically advanced, and best financed companies in the country. And even some of these have not succeeded, as was shown by the partial or complete failure of General Foods, Colgate, Gillette, Otis, Honeywell, and others.[8] There is little room for smaller firms that make ordinary products and have little excess cash. These firms are the bulk of the enterprises in any country and, despite their limitations, many are able to export elsewhere. Until they also get a crack at the Japanese market, it would be hard to claim that this market is accessible.

ALTERING THE SYSTEM

Before dealing with how the situation is changing and whether other countries have the right to militate for more change, it is necessary to dispose of one important point: Are the *keiretsu* a form of discrimination against foreign products and companies?

Throughout the description of the various groupings, repeated reference has been made to the "insiders," which benefit from these ties, and the "outsiders," which lose. But it would be incorrect to assume that "outsiders" is equivalent to foreigners. Domestic companies that are not part of any group face the same difficulties. Being Japanese—as opposed to being American, German, or French—is immaterial. In this narrow sense, there is no true discrimination based on the origin of a company or product.

Also, for the outsiders, including foreign entities, there are advantages as well as drawbacks. While it is harder to deal with any given group, it is easier to approach a wider circle of clients (which could include members of several groups) because the traditional suspicion and rivalry do not apply to outsiders. If they have a useful product or technology, it could be picked up in any part of the market. This, of course, is not quite as great an advantage as having ready access to a specific group, enjoying the financial and marketing support it provides, and knowing that there is a foundation on which to build. But it is an advantage nonetheless. Whether it outweighs the advantages of operating in a truly open market—namely, one in which there are no major groupings or the groupings cannot regulate commercial flows as much as they do—is another matter.

It could hardly be denied that if all companies were equal, if they started from the same point, and products were sold purely on the basis of price, quality, service, and so on, things would be better. This ideal situation could be urged upon Japan to avoid any feeling of unfairness. Since this is the avowed goal of the Japanese government, it might be argued that foreign countries have the right to protest about difficulties that arise.

Whether this is proper or not is a moot point. Foreign governments have been protesting and are bound to do so more in the future. After all, if liberalization in all others aspects of tariffs, quotas, standards, and so forth does not restore the trade balance, a second look will be directed toward the distribution sector. It will be much harder to intervene here, since this involves indigenous customs, practices, and relationships. But they will certainly come under closer scrutiny.[9]

Fortunately, there are several trends that augur well for the future. They are part of relatively spontaneous movements within the business community or state, and could go far to alter the present situation.

One of these developments is the tendency of members of the horizontal groupings, the formidable *keiretsu*, to go their own way more and more. The two core companies in most cases are the bank and the *sogo shosha*. Banks, while always useful, have become less crucial over the years. There are other sources of funds. The trading companies have also slipped somewhat. Bulk commodities, in which they specialize, are less essential and they have not done as well in handling smaller lots of finished products.

This relaxation can be seen in various ways. Member companies now turn more to other banks, including foreign ones. They also export their own products and sometimes import raw materials directly. The crossholding has tended to fall in the major groups, although only slightly so far. Meetings of presidents are regarded as somewhat ritualistic and have less impact on day-to-day operations. Aside from some new sectors, not many joint projects are being launched. This is hardly the dusk of the *keiretsu*, but it does leave more openings for outsiders.

Unfortunately, relations within the vertical groupings have become more intense than ever. With the harsh economic climate, more and more suppliers and subcontractors, including some that were relatively independent, have turned to the parent companies for financial or management assistance. In order to survive in an increasingly competitive market, the parent companies have also imposed stricter control on quality, delivery, and price. Meanwhile, innovations like computerization and robotization make it easier to know just what the lesser members are doing and work them more deeply into the team.

The situation for the distribution *keiretsu* is mixed. On the one hand, the parent companies have sometimes reinforced the integration of retailers by acquiring more of their stock or offering more credit. Some that might otherwise have failed were bought up. Yet, this has become such a heavy burden that certain groups, including Toyota, are gradually withdrawing and urging their dealers to be more independent. At the same time, in some sectors there has been an increase in the number of independent stores that sell a variety of brands, some of which have become remarkably successful by combining the broader choice with lower prices or better terms.

The most encouraging change, however, has been the spectacular rise of chain stores. Once far behind the department stores, they now account for about 12 percent of all retail sales. These chains have grown tremendously, as has the turnover, which makes it increasingly possible for chain stores to import goods directly and distribute them through their own outlets. This is further aided by the fact that the chains are parts of groups that also have department stores, convenience stores, specialty stores, and so on. This makes them potentially the biggest and best channel.[10]

At this point, it is necessary to consider a very different kind of influence. This is exerted by the Fair Trade Commission, which is Japan's antitrust agency. Established under the Antimonopoly Act of 1947, it has had its share of vicissitudes. During the boom years of the 1950s and 1960s, it was weakened by various revisions and government policies. With the recession, however, it was strengthened by a new revision in 1977. Presently, acting under the mandate, it has been reasonably vigorous in its surveillance of an occasional action against groupings.

The FTC's interests are not strictly the same as those of foreign companies or governments. It has to prevent excessive concentration of sales resulting in monopoly or oligopoly, as well as check that collusion between firms does not cause unwarranted price hikes. One of the FTC's primary concerns is to prevent the practice of resale price maintenance by the manufacturers imposed through the distribution keiretsu.[11]

Nonetheless, the FTC's exercises are of interest. For example, to avoid excessive concentration it has had legislation passed or adopted guidelines to limit the shareholding of banks in all other companies, including group companies. It has also limited, albeit at somewhat higher levels, the shareholding of manufacturers in rival firms.[12] This has loosened the groups somewhat.

While it cannot intervene in dealings between group members in ordinary circumstances, the FTC definitely has to act when cartels are formed. This includes not only sales cartels, which existed most notoriously for the purchase of soda ash, but also, in varying degrees, imports of pulp and paper, aluminum ingots, petroleum, and so on. Prevention of such collusion and dissolution of the cartels are certainly to the good of foreign companies.

The FTC's primary concerns with distribution keiretsu are the price maintenance arrangements and the abuse of rebates to tie in retailers; putting an end to both practices would again loosen the group. This could be a decisive step if it were followed up, as has sometimes been hinted, by an energetic campaign to restore independence to the retailers and dealers. No longer bound by law or by debt to their parent company or one large manufacturer, outlets could begin selling the products of several manufacturers. Automobile dealers might sell several makes of cars.

Just how far the Fair Trade Commission will go is uncertain, and many of these promises may not be fulfilled. After all, as noted, the FTC's interests do not necessarily coincide with those of foreign exporters and manufacturers. Moreover, it is part of the Japanese political structure and must do the bidding of the party in power. Given the Liberal Democratic Party's close ties with business circles, it could run into trouble if it went too far. This is scarcely an academic point, since the Japan Federation of Economic Organizations (Keidanren), the bastion of big business, has been complaining about the FTC's actions and urging a further revision of the Antimonopoly Act, this time to restrict the FTC.[13]

Perhaps realizing this, the Fair Trade Commission has carefully refrained from undertaking action that could be interpreted as playing into the hands of foreigners. Not only that, it has issued various studies of the Japanese market that conclude that it is "open" and "not unfair."[14] That these studies were often vitiated by too narrow a focus or systematic neglect of contrary evidence is interesting. But what is more significant is that it would be naive to regard the FTC as a useful tool or of more than indirect help here.

This means that foreign governments that wish to have the situation improved will probably have to continue working as in the past. They will have to make remonstrations to the Japanese government, show how specific practices cause specific difficulties, and then request that something be done to remedy that. As noted, it will not be easy. It is not usual to complain about local business practices that are frequently quite idiosyncratic, even when they are effective barriers. This is obviously not covered by GATT. But, if they are ignored, little can be achieved.

Foreign governments are probably on somewhat more solid ground when they complain about practices that, even if customary, are also a violation of Japan's own laws. This signifies primarily conduct that is forbidden by the Antimonopoly Act, whether or not uncovered and prosecuted by the Fair Trade Commission. Certainly, there is every cause to object to cartels, including those that arise from the activities of the Ministry of International Trade and Industry.[15] It might also seem appropriate to investigate the refusal of retailers or dealers to carry competing products, should a foreign maker care to lodge such a charge.

Whatever the case, it is essential for foreign trade negotiators to know exactly how the groupings operate and where they are in contradiction of the law of the land so that less time will be wasted on futile debates over what is "fair" and "unfair." Every country, every business community has its own ideas on that matter. Breaches of national legislation are another thing entirely and, at a minimum, Japan should be held to its own laws.

NOTES

1. See Senjuro Takahashi, "Is the Distribution System a Trade Barrier?" *Economic Eye*, June, 1983, pp. 19–24.

2. See Dentsu Incorporated, *Marketing Opportunities in Japan*, Tuttle, Tokyo, 1978, pp. 53–83.

3. Ibid.

4. See Zimmerman, op. cit., pp. 218–35.

5. See Fumio Mikuriya, "Distribution: The Key to Success in the Japanese Market," *The Wheel Extended*, Summer, 1980, pp. 17–22.

6. See Kinya Ninomiya, "Foreign Firms' Strategies in Japan," *Oriental Economist*, November, 1980, pp. 16–21.

7. Ibid.

8. See "Successes and Failures of Foreign Firms in Japan," *Oriental Economist,* June, 1985.

9. See Woronoff, *World Trade War,* Praeger, New York, 1984, pp. 218–36.

10. See Dodwell, *The Structure of the Japanese Retail and Distribution Industry,* Tokyo, 1985.

11. See Ishida, op cit..

12. The limits are 10 percent (and later 5 percent) in the former case and 50 percent in the latter.

13. See, among others, Chihaya Kawade, "Antimonopoly Law, FTC in Need of Reform," *Keidanren Review,* October, 1983, pp. 5–9.

14. See Fair Trade Commission, *The Fair Trade Commission's Approach to Trade Friction,* April, 1983.

15. The FTC has repeatedly criticized MITI's antirecession cartels and other arrangements, but without acting thus far.

Part III
THE DISTRIBUTION MAZE

10

Distribution As
A Market Factor

This section focuses on the Japanese distribution system. In addition to the cultural and business impact of the *keiretsu*, it is the distribution system that has led to many nontariff barrier accusations against Japan, and is perceived by a number of analysts and many business executives to be Japan's primary barrier to imports.[1]

Western observers frequently refer to Japan's traditional distribution system as "mysterious, complex, archaic, old fashioned, stubborn, inefficient and anachronistic."[2] Often, however, the Japanese distribution system continues to be perceived today as it was 20 years ago. Anecdotal evidence appears to posess a particularly long life-span—often exceeding by far the public's capability to retain facts. It is the purpose of this part of the book to present a current view of the Japanese distribution system. In doing so, it aims to accomplish three major objectives. First, it will describe the Japanese distribution system, with a particular focus on consumer products. It will discuss the structure of Japanese distribution channel, highlight unique characteristics of the distribution process, and show how historical factors contributed to this uniqueness. Second, an overview of the current innovations and changes taking place in the distribution system is presented. Third, conclusions will be drawn about the meaning and the impact of these changes to business executives and policymakers.

In approaching these objectives, particular attention will be paid to comparing the Japanese and U.S. systems of distribution. Major emphasis will also rest on assessing the importation of consumer products into Japan, and on ways to increase the success of such products in Japan.

71

Various limitations and constraints of this work should be called to the attention of the reader. When considering the breadth of import relations of a nation (as outlined in Figure 10.1), four major playing fields exist. These are the exporting country under study, the transfer process of exports, the importing country, and third countries which are exposed to repercussions. Within each of these areas, due to different concerns, a segmentation along type of import is necessary, with a segmentation into commodities, industrial goods, consumer products, and services representing a rough but adequate generalization. Subsequently, for each area and each type of import, a differentiation of private and public sector activities is needed that can in turn be subdivided into import (export) inhibiting or encouraging. Each one of these subdivisions then raises issues such as financing, distribution, research, and so forth. Given this framework of necessary areas for a complete study of export (import) relations between two countries, the reader must be aware that this volume addresses mainly the area of consumer products within Japan, with a major focus on private sector activity in the field of distribution. In this context, it must be remembered that consumer products comprise only a small portion of U.S.-Japanese trade (see Table 10.1). Even though the value of U.S. consumer product exports to Japan has been increasing steadily, in 1983 these products represented only 6.4 percent of U.S. imports to Japan. The major U.S.-Japanese trade frictions and negotiations have focused on commodities and industrial products, with services gradually emerging as an additional important issue. By the same token, however, it can be argued that more attention needs to be focused on increasing exports of U.S. consumer products to Japan, particularly since "consumer goods exporters [to Japan] experience the greatest frustration because of their exposure to different layers of the [distribution] system."[3]

A second major caveat for the reader should be the fact that this work represents the findings of a small-scale, exploratory study. In addition to the customary (and extensive) literature review, the findings presented here are the result of facts and opinions gathered from policymakers and business executives in both the United States and Japan. For purposes of this study, meetings and interviews were conducted with 97 individuals from 51 public and private sector institutions.

IMPORT TYPE	CONSUMER PRODUCTS	INDUSTRIAL PRODUCTS	COMMODITIES	SERVICES
Locus of Issue				
Exporting Country	PUBLIC SECTOR obstacles + encouragements			
	PRIVATE SECTOR obstacles + encouragements			
Transfer	PUBLIC SECTOR obstacles + encouragements			
	PRIVATE SECTOR obstacles + encouragements			
Importing Country	PUBLIC SECTOR obstacles + encouragements,			
	PRIVATE SECTOR obstacles + encouragements, distribution, financing			
Third Country Repercussions	PUBLIC SECTOR obstacles + encouragements			
	PRIVATE SECTOR obstacles + encouragements			

FIGURE 10.1. Framework for the Study of Import Relations between Two Nations.

The U.S. portion of the work was supported by the National Center for Export-Import Studies at Georgetown University, a nonprofit, nonpartisan research organization. The research in Japan was arranged and funded by the Japanese Ministry for International Trade and Industry (MITI), the Japan External Trade Organization (JETRO), and the Distribution Systems Research Institute.

Time constraints did not allow for interaction with some participants in the Japan distribution system—for example,

TABLE 10.1. U.S. Exports to Japan (U.S. $ million)

	Total Exports		Consumer Goods*		Industrial Goods	
	Value	Pct.	Value	Pct.	Value	Pct.
1965	2.084	100	0.074	3.6	0.872	41.8
1970	4.625	100	0.213	4.6	2.119	45.6
1975	9.565	100	0.509	5.3	4.294	44.9
1980	20.790	100	1.154	5.6	9.500	45.7
1981	21.823	100	1.318	6.0	8.983	41.2
1982	20.966	100	1.356	6.5	9.173	43.8
1983	21.894	100	1.394	6.4	8.734	39.9

Source: FT 990, Highlights of U.S. Exports-Imports, U.S. Bureau of the Census, Washington, D.C., 1984, p. 47.

*Durables and nondurables, except automotive

manufacturers or the famed *sogo shoshas*, and the method of research permitted mainly the gathering of qualitative rather than quantitative data. The exposure, however, was sufficiently in-depth to permit for the presentation of some important insights into the Japanese distribution system.

NOTES

1. Raymond J. Ahern, "Market Access in Japan: The U.S. Experience," Congressional Research Service, Report No. 85–37E, February 14, 1985.

2. Mitsuaki Shimaguchi and William Lazer, "Japanese Distribution Channels: Invisible Barriers to Market Entry," *MSU Business Topics*, Winter, 1979, Vol. 27, No. 1, p. 51.

3. "Strategies for Alleviating Recurrent Bilateral Trade Problems between Japan and the United States," in *The Japanese Non-Tariff Trade Barrier Issue: American Views and Implications for Japan-U.S. Trade Relations*, Report to the Japanese National Institute for Research Advancement, Arthur D. Little, Inc., May, 1979, pp. 4–52.

11

Origins And Development

Most studies of the Japanese market that deal with the importation of products make extensive reference to the country's complex and unique distribution system. They frequently mention the multilayered channel structure and the fact that wholesalers (or *tonya*) keep on selling to each other, and they highlight the atomistic competition among retailers. As one report notes, Japan has a vast distribution network "with more wholesalers and retailers per capita than any other of the advanced industrial nations."[1] Another study finds that "the manner in which the Japanese channels of distribution are structured and managed presents one of the major reasons for the apparent failure of foreign firms to establish major market participation in Japan."[2]

It needs to be kept in mind, however, that distribution systems usually develop in a certain way for a logical reason. The current system has developed because it represents the "most economical and efficient means of serving [the] market environment."[3] Before embarking on a description of the current system, it therefore seems appropriate to trace briefly the historical development of the Japanese distribution system in order to attain a better understanding of today's realities.

During the feudal period of Japan, the country consisted of many small provinces that were largely self-contained. As a result, each province developed its own distribution system. Even after the abandonment of feudalism, the individuality and uniqueness of these provinces largely remained. Manufacturers who wished to penetrate these areas successfully had to develop appropriate distribution systems for each area. Since Japan consisted of about 500 regions, many manufacturers needed to develop wholesalers for each territory.

In addition to the feudal system, and perhaps of even more profound relevance, is the fact that the four main island divisions of Japan have restricted the mobility of people and merchandise. As a result, suppliers needed to work with intermediaries in each of these areas since they were far better able to deal with customers in often remote places.

Over time, these constraints resulted in a system characterized by many small manufacturers who, in order to survive, needed the financing, distribution, and storage capabilities provided by wholesalers. These manufacturers were in need of middlemen to market their products widely. By using a multilayered channel system, their products could be marketed at "a fraction of the costs of direct sales."[4] Direct sales by manufacturers would result in a logistical nightmare, since they would require an astronomical number of contacts and deliveries. As the concept of channel geometry presented in Figure 11.1 shows, the use of intermediaries resulted in an additive, rather than a multiplicative, number of contacts and deliveries. Considering the number of manufacturers and retailers involved, this difference is of enormous significance. Rationally, the intermediary is positively contributing to the economic process, as long as its charges for services are less than the savings incurred by the manufacturers due to the reduction of contacts.

Another reason for the current distribution system is the fact that Japanese manufacturers, in line with the general tendency toward specialization and division of labor, often preferred to specialize in their area of expertise, which is production, not distribution. Because of these factors, manufacturers and wholesalers frequently have made exclusive contracts.

Retailers in turn, being numerous, very small, and confined to very specific geographic regions, needed the inventory and distribution functions provided by wholesalers in order to survive. Again, this resulted in close relationships between retailers and wholesalers.

Other social developments contributed to the existence and expansion of small retailers who were dependent upon wholesalers. Japanese society has come to accept to some degree a "tolerated inefficiency" within its distribution system in order to maintain employment and income flows. Retailing has come to serve to some extent as a "form of social welfare system."[5]

A. Direct Delivery by Manufacturers (3 Manufacturers, 10 Retailers)

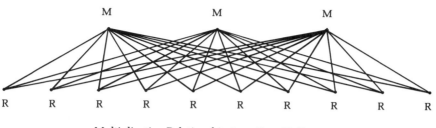

Multiplicative Relationship 3 × 10 = 30 Contacts

B. Delivery Via Wholesale Intermediary

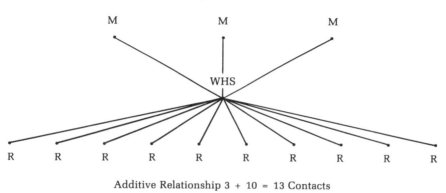

Additive Relationship 3 + 10 = 13 Contacts

FIGURE 11.1. Channel Geometry Effects on the Distribution System

Since Japanese employees at retirement are paid a lump sum rather than an ongoing pension, this payment is often seen by the individual as an opportunity to set up a shop in order to be independent and to derive a steady income. As retirement often occurs at an early age, relative to other industrialized countries, maintenance of income is important. The limited capital and experience of these retailers increase their dependence on wholesalers.

In addition to the interdependence among channel members as a Japanese way of life, which results in bonds forged by mutual obligation and service, there are other reasons for the current decentralized distribution system:

- The financial needs of a system in which most business is done on the basis of promissory notes, debt financing, and consignments
- The need for risk reduction in distribution, which is achieved by the sharing of responsibility
- Specific system features such as rebates, discounts, and the unquestioned return of unsold goods
- The need to keep inventory constantly moving throughout the system
- The need to keep goods moving rapidly from producers to consumers[6]
- The expected long-term commitment by channel members in terms of time, money, and personnel, and the expected willingness for large investments devoted toward market entry with only a very limited return
- A system emphasis on secure and steady supply[7]
- Restrictions and limitations of retailers existing mainly in the areas of space and capital
- The existing geographic limitations. Since migration patterns have resulted in a concentration of populations in cities, narrow and congested streets require small-lot deliveries in small vehicles.

Within all these constraints, a distribution system has developed that is fulfilling the demands placed on it. Functions are clearly distributed, as shown in the example in Figure 11.2. Manufacturers concentrate mainly on production and national promotional activities. Intermediaries interact closely with both the manufacturing and the retailing level; their work extends far beyond pure break bulk or product assortment activities. Retailers in turn concentrate on selling and promotional activities aimed at consumers within their area of business.

All the facets of the distribution system outlined so far will continually resurface in the remainder of this section. This short discussion was intended to delineate more clearly the historical growth of the Japanese distribution system and to demonstrate that, although due to its multilayered structure and its many uniquely Japanese procedural facets foreign entry into this market may be perceived as tedious and difficult, this appears to be mainly the result of systemic constraints that, to a large extent, apply equally well to domestic products.

COSMETICS INDUSTRY
CHANNEL MEMBER

Manufacturer	*Intermediary*	*Retail*
Production	Order taking	Selling
Advertising	Inventory Maintenance	Organize Consumers
National Sales Promotion	Space Control at the Retail Level	In-store Promotion
Dealer Aids	Product Assortment	
Education of Dealers	Dispatching of Sales Support Personnel	
Financing	Area Marketing	
	Financing	

FIGURE 11.2.   An Example of Function Performance
in the Channel System

Source: Interview with executives of Chuo Bussan K.K. (Central
Distributors, Inc.), Tokyo, March, 1984.

NOTES

1. "Japanese Barriers to U.S. Trade and Recent Japanese Government Trade Initiatives," *Office of the United States Trade Representative,* Washington, D.C., 1982, p. 71.

2. E. Ross Randolph, "Understanding the Japanese Distribution System: Explanatory Framework," *European Journal of Marketing,* Vol. 17, No. 1, 1983, p. 12.

3. Yoshi Tsurumi, "Managing Consumer and Industrial Systems in Japan," *Sloan Management Review,* Fall, 1982, p. 42.

4. Ibid.

5. "Strategies for Alleviating Recurrent Bilateral Trade Problems between Japan and the United States," in *The Japanese Non-Tariff Trade Barrier Issue: American Views and Implications for Japan-U.S. Trade Relations,* Report to the Japanese National Institute for Research Advancement, Arthur D. Little, Inc., May, 1979, pp. 4–49.

6. Ibid., pp. 4–51.

7. Office of the United States Trade Representative, op. cit., p. 71.

12

Wholesaling
In Japan

This chapter will highlight the wholesaling activities taking place in Japan. Initially, the focus will rest with the wholesale structure, with a particular emphasis on channel members. Subsequently, the wholesaling process will be discussed—that is, the performance of the wholesaling function.

THE WHOLESALING STRUCTURE

Wholesalers in Japan are oriented mainly, although not exclusively, along functional, geographic, and product dimensions.[1] Functional wholesalers take on very specific roles as either export or import wholesalers or as primary, secondary, or even tertiary wholesalers. Geographic orientation expresses itself by a national or regional focus. Product orientation is often based on regional comparative advantage due to manufacturing concentration on particular product categories such as kimonos, pearls, or frames for glasses—much like, for example, the garment district in Manhattan or the diamond district in Amsterdam.

Frequently, "wholesalers have a dominant position in the Japanese economy and have played a vital link in the selling chain for small manufacturers and retailers."[2] However, this holds true only for cases of low levels of concentration on the retail or manufacturing level. Conversely, in situations where concentration exists—as is the case, for example, in the electrical appliance industry, which has only a small number of major manufacturers—systematized forms of distribution controlled by the manufacturers exist, often in the form of manufacturers sales centers, thus excluding or at least reducing the role of the wholesalers.

To manufacturers, "wholesalers have traditionally supplied managerial or marketing knowhow as well as financial assistance to procure raw materials."[3] In addition, wholesalers are instrumental in performing break bulk functions in order to service the many small retailers who cannot order minimum-size quantities from manufacturers, as they have insufficient storage space (due to high land prices, the cost of storage space is unaffordable). Wholesalers, particularly the older and more established firms, are at an advantage with regard to retailers and to new entrants into the wholesaling market, since they already have land and buildings that were acquired at lower prices and frequently have already been depreciated. Retailers' lack of storage space has resulted in a need for frequent replenishments. Since these replenishments are expected to be delivered rapidly, a need for close wholesaler proximity to retailers has arisen. This in turn has led to the development of large numbers of small wholesalers who are served by larger wholesalers.

In 1979, the latest year for which data are available, Japan had over 368,000 wholesalers. Table 12.1 provides a breakdown of wholesalers by area of concentration in Japan. As can be seen, wholesale establishments are concentrated in the two prefectures of Tokyo and Osaka. These areas combined contain more than 28 percent of all Japanese wholesalers, with Tokyo having the clear lead with a 17.7 percent share of all wholesalers. Comparatively, all other regions drop off sharply in the extent of their wholesale activities.

A comparison between the Japanese and the U.S. wholesale structure (shown in Table 12.2) results in a number of interesting findings. Japan and the United States have roughly the same number of wholesalers, even though the United States is substantially larger than Japan. Total annual sales of the wholesaling sector and average annual sales per wholesaler are also quite similar between the two. The population per wholesaler, however, is substantially lower in Japan than in the United States, as can be expected with the U.S. population almost twice that of Japan. Wholesalers in both countries serve between 4.5 and 5 retailers on the average. This fact does not reflect, however, the difference in size of retailers, a point that will be expanded on in the section

TABLE 12.1. Wholesalers in Japan

Area of Concentration	No. of Establishments	Percentage
Tokyo	65,324	17.72
Osaka	40,203	10.90
Aichi	25,561	6.93
Fukuoka	15,725	4.27
Hokkaido	15,721	4.26
Hyogo	13,509	3.66
Kanagawa	12,820	3.48
Shizhuoka	10,825	2.94
Hiroshima	10,410	2.82
Saitama	9,767	2.65
Chiba	8,405	2.28
Others	140,416	38.09
Total	368,686	100.00

Source: *Statistics of Commerce*, Ministry of International Trade and Industry, 1980.

on retailing structure. The number of employees per wholesaler also appears to be remarkably similar. One must remember, however, that the Japanese computations include the very large trading houses or *sogo shoshas*, which, due to their large employment, may distort the picture somewhat. As can be seen in Table 12.3 more than 46 percent of Japanese wholesalers are small, having less than four employees. Large wholesalers, having 30 or more employees, comprise only 5.6 percent of the total number of establishments. These figures, which clearly show that Japanese wholesalers tend to be fairly small, are corroborated by studies that indicate that most wholesalers have less than nine employees.[4]

A comparison between combined wholesale and retail sales in Japan and the United States is presented in Table 12.4. This reveals that the ratio of wholesale to retail sales in Japan is more than double that of the United States. The ratio of wholesalers to retailers could be adjusted for more accuracy by deducting industrial transactions in which merchandise customarily flows directly from wholesalers to end-users. While doing so would

TABLE 12.2.   A Comparison between the Japanese
and the U.S. Wholesale Structure

	Japan (1979)	U.S. (1977)
Number of Wholesalers	369,000.0	383,000.0
Number of Employees	3,688,000.0	4,376,000.0
Total Annual Sales (Dollars, Million)	1,244,000.0*	1,258,000.0
Annual Sales per Wholesaler (Dollars, Million)	3.4	3.3
Population per Wholesaler	351.0	643.0
Number of Employees per Wholesaler	10.0	11.4
Number of Retailers per Wholesaler	4.5	4.8

*Calculated at 223 yen = 1 US $

Sources: For Japan data: Statistics of Commerce, Ministry of International Trade and Industry, 1979. For U.S. data: Statistical Abstract of the U.S., 1984 Edition, U.S. Department of Commerce, Washington, D.C., 1984.

TABLE 12.3.   The Size of Japanese Wholesalers in 1979

Number of Employees	Number of Establishments	Percentage
Small sized (1-4)	171,569	46.5
Medium sized (5-29)	176,356	47.9
Large sized (30 and over)	20,761	5.6
Total	368,686	100.0

Source: Commercial Census, 1979, Ministry of International Trade and Industry.

reduce the ratio for Japan to approximately 2 to 1, a similar adjustment for the U.S. data would still result in the Japanese ratio of wholesalers to retailers being more than twice as high as the U.S. one.

THE WHOLESALING PROCESS

Japanese wholesale distribution is characterized by very close ties between the participants in the distribution process:

TABLE 12.4. Comparison of Wholesale Sales and Retail Sales in the United States and Japan (U.S. $ billion)

	Japan (1979)	U.S. (1977)
Combined wholesale sales	1,244	1,258
Combined retail sales	330	725
Ratio wholesale: retail	3.77:1	1.74:1

Sources: For Japan data: Statistics of Commerce, Ministry of International Trade and Industry, 1979. For U.S. data: Statistical Abstract of the U.S., 1984 Edition, U.S. Department of Commerce, Washington, D.C. 1984.

the manufacturers, the various levels of wholesalers, and the retailers. While these close ties may to some extent be the result of business interdependence, they are also a function of close personal relationships that are expressed through frequent visits and elaborate courtesies. The maintenance of this relationship is often far more important than the sales level of a particular product or short-term profitability. It includes the occasional provision of money to "send the son to school," frequent exchanges of gifts, friendly discussions, and very little direct pressure to sell. Violation of this relationship can have quite negative repercussions, as one U.S. supplier found out when his sales agreement with a large distributor was terminated. The Japanese distributor explained later that "when the U.S. sales manager visited some of my retail clients, not only did he keep on badgering them on how they had to increase sales, but he even refused to bow to them during the welcome greeting. He never understood the importance of our relationship, and that the retailers were really doing him a favor by carrying his product." Understanding these relationships and becoming part of them are therefore imperative for any firm wanting to do business successfully in Japan.

The existence of these strong bonds, however, should not be interpreted as doing away with competition. Wholesalers are expected by their retailers to be actively involved in business development, and pressures are exerted via them on the manufacturers to remain competitive in their product offerings.

The importance of the relationship among channel members is perhaps best highlighted with the example of a new product introduction. Often, such newly introduced products require the development of an entirely new distribution system. Even if this is not the case, the difficulty faced by firms new to the market is how to displace established products, particularly since space constraints are a major factor in the Japanese channel. As a result, national introduction of a new product is quite expensive and time-consuming. The process frequently starts out with meetings across the country between the manufacturer (or importer) and some of the major wholesaling groups. (A listing of these groups is in the Appendix at the end of this chapter.) These meetings—which often take the form of parties for presenting the product, receiving channel input on marketing plans, and, most important, establishing or maintaining channel relationships—usually cost around $130,000. The creation of a TV advertisement will cost approximately $85,000, with a subsequent annual national advertising budget of $1.3 million. Total introductory costs can therefore easily approach $1.5 to $2.2 million. While this cost may appear high, the manufacturer must incur it in order to obtain the cooperation of channel members.

For channel members to accept a new product, the manufacturer has to pursue both a push and a pull strategy. In instances of highly visible or desirable goods, channel members may be willing to share some of the introductory costs, but the manufacturer must bear most of these expenses. These initial expenses, however, do not guarantee success. Japanese wholesalers believe it is important for manufacturers to follow up continuously on a first success of a product by improving it. If such improvements are not forthcoming, competitors are likely to enter the market with similar but lower-priced products, and the initial introductory success will be short-lived.

This is particularly the case for imports, since the emergence of a competitive Japanese product may result in current wholesalers of the imported product returning to their long-standing Japanese suppliers and dropping the imported product. The U.S. manufacturers of Odoreaters experienced such a development. After three years of quite costly market development efforts together with a Japanese wholesaler, the firm had reached a sales level of 3.8 million pairs. However, six months after product introduction, 12 comparable Japanese products had already been introduced. Since Odoreaters was not able to improve its product substantially over time, its wholesaler made an exclusive agreement with a competing firm—Scholl, Inc.— and terminated the relationship with Odoreaters. Even though Odoreaters found another distributor, its sales have dropped significantly.

Polaroid went through a similar experience. It had to change wholesalers after Fuji Photo Film introduced its instant camera because Polaroid could no longer depend upon Fuji Photo Film-affiliated wholesalers to act as its distributors.[5]

Once a product is successfully established, wholesalers are expected to supply a substantial amount of sales-support personnel for their products to retailers. This support staff often works in the retail store, wearing the store uniforms, but paid for by the wholesaler. In some department store areas, wholesaler-supplied personnel vastly outnumber store-employed personnel. In one case, 95 percent of the staff in the cosmetic section of a store consisted of outside employees. The rationale behind this practice is that it is in the interest of the wholesaler (or manufacturer) to have personnel pushing its products, since its personnel is better able to explain the products to customers.

Wholesalers are also expected to offer a very liberal return privilege to retailers, which extends not only to damaged merchandise but also to merchandise that does not sell easily. This privilege exists mainly to help small stores that cannot afford to keep unsold products in their limited space for long.[6]

One of the major reasons for the existence of wholesalers of course is the lack of storage and warehousing facilities in Japan. Even though the Japanese government has begun to introduce change by making warehousing facilities more widely available (a phenomenon that will be discussed in a later chapter), the cost of storage space is very high. In order to obtain space in an existing distribution center, tenants often need to pay a number of charges on a square-meter basis. Examples of these changes are:

- Construction contribution fund: a one-time payment that is refundable only after ten years with no interest payment, amounts to approximately $200 per square meter.
- Security deposit: refundable only at the end of the lease with no interest paid. This deposit is approximately $500 per square meter
- Monthly rent: $12.50 per square meter
- Administrative charges: $4 per square meter

Leases typically need to be signed for a minimum term of ten years. Despite these substantial costs, vacancy rates at distribution centers are extremely low, with outside turnover often being less than 2 percent. These required long-term commitments to storage space are not seen as onerous by Japanese firms, since the entire distribution structure rests on the notion of long-term commitments of ten years and more between channel members.

Due to the lack of storage space and its high cost, delivery lead time takes on a major significance in the wholesaling process. Suppliers, particularly those from abroad, are chosen on the basis of responsiveness to orders by wholesalers. Even when sophisticated sales forecasting systems are used, immediate manufacturer response to short-term orders is expected. As a result, factors such as short lead time and secure suppliers often can outweigh price competiveness.

The financing activities of wholesalers also play a major role in the distribution process. Extended payment terms prevail in the wholesaling sector, with promissory notes frequently used for 90 to 120 days. In addition to straight financing, wholesalers are also deeply involved in maintaining an elaborate system of rebates.[7] Wholesalers, acting as agents for manufacturers, frequently receive commissions or rebates of 2 to 5 percent for invoicing and collecting from the channel members. These commissions can be lower if the product is better known. Larger wholesalers can also receive a rebate based on performance, very similar to a cumulative discount, that often ranges between 1 and 3 percent. For quick payment (within 30 days), 3 percent cash payment discounts are frequently granted. Wholesalers are also rewarded by manufacturers for controlling disorderly markets by, for example, reducing aggressive discounting by retailers. Such rebates often are as high as 2 percent. Quantity discounts are also granted for certain sizes of minimum orders and usually range between 1 and 2 percent. While wholesalers can easily accumulate up to a 10 percent discount this way from manufacturers, parts of these rebates need to be passed on to retailers. Retailers, for example, may receive payments for being cooperative, for example, by staying below an expected level of returned goods. Retailers may also receive payments for quantity purchases and for participation in displays. Annual bonuses paid by wholesalers to retailers can be 2 to 3 percent, and are often passed-on payments that have previously been made for this specific purpose by the manufacturer to the wholesaler.

As can be expected, various distribution routes may exist for similar goods. The choice of a suitable channel of distribution results from considerations of product characteristics, market characteristics, consumer purchasing behavior, and size and competitive position of the firm. These considerations also affect wholesale activities. For example, not all wholesalers engage in distribution activities; some mainly consolidate products and forward them to the large consumption centers to be distributed there. Other regionally specialized wholesalers offer mainly a credit function without having a distribution network. Figure 12.1 provides an example of such different distribution alternatives, using the case of soap.

Case 1 presents the most frequently used channel (60 percent of soap is distributed this way). Product deliveries are made from the manufacturer to a wholesaler, who in turn delivers to a retailer. Payment flows go from the retailer to the wholesaler, who in turn pays the manufacturer.

Case 2 demonstrates another frequently used distribution process. Wholesaler A sells the product to the smaller wholesaler B. Product flow, however, goes directly from the manufacturer to wholesaler B. Wholesaler B in turn delivers to the retailer. The fact that wholesaler B rather than A deals with the retailer can be ascribed to the fact that B frequently has the older and longer business relationship with the retailer. Similarly, due to established relationships, B is more likely to deal with A rather than going directly to the manufacturer. Payment flows go from the retailer to wholesaler B, who in turn pays wholesaler A, who forwards payment to the manufacturer. Even though wholesaler A has not handled any of the physical product flow, it will receive a 5 percent commission on the sale from the manufacturer.

In Case 3, the channel is expanded by the addition of a very small wholesaler C. This wholesaler, even though virtually unknown to the manufacturer, receives its delivery of goods directly from the manufacturer. However, the manufacturer is willing to make this delivery only if wholesaler A guarantees the payment. Wholesaler A is able to do so because of its long established relationship with wholesaler B, who in turn main-

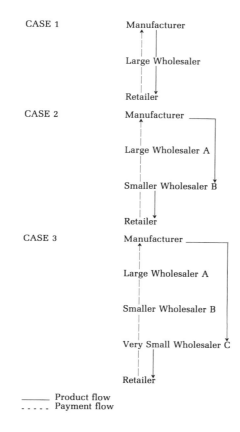

CASE 1

Manufacturer

Large Wholesaler

Retailer

CASE 2

Manufacturer

Large Wholesaler A

Smaller Wholesaler B

Retailer

CASE 3

Manufacturer

Large Wholesaler A

Smaller Wholesaler B

Very Small Wholesaler C

Retailer

——— Product flow
- - - - Payment flow

FIGURE 12.1. Variety of Distribution Alternatives—
The Channels for Soap

tains a trusted relationship with wholesaler C. The very small
wholesaler in turn is able to deliver to retailers who often are
quite far removed from any possible reach of the manufacturer
(for example, a beach sales shop). Due to all these interlinkages,
the manufacturer has ensured wide distribution of its product
while minimizing the risk of nonpayment. The different
wholesalers in turn have not incurred major expenditures since
they have not participated in handling the physical product flow.
In exchange for their credit facilitation, however, they are able to
participate in the profits from the sale.

In summary, it can be said that wholesaling in Japan is characterized by the following salient dimensions:

- major importance of traditional ties
- significant focus on service support throughout the channel
- important role of credit and financing
- sharing of risk and responsibility
- emphasis on rapid delivery and secure supplies.

APPENDIX

Major Japanese Wholesaling Groups

Abe Shoji Group	Shin Nihon Shoji Group
Fujisan Shokai Group	Terauchi Group
Itokin Group	Toho Yakuhin Group
Matsumo Jitsugyo Group	Tsukuda Group
Nakaizumi Group	Yamasan Group
Sanpo Shoji Group	Yoshichu Group

Source: Compiled by authors from: *The Structure of the Japanese Retail and Distribution Industry, 1981/82*, Dodwell Marketing Consultants, Tokyo, 1981, pp. 101–09.

NOTES

1. William Lazer, Shoji Murata, and Hiroshi Kosaka, "Japanese Marketing: Towards a Better Understanding," *Journal of Marketing*, Vol. 49, No. 2, 1985, pp. 69–81.

2. *The Structure of the Japanese Retail and Distribution Industry 1981/82*, Dodwell Marketing Consultants, Tokyo, 1981, p. 71.

3. Ibid., p. 13.

4. Yoshi Tsurumi, "Managing Consumer and Industrial Systems in Japan," *Sloan Management Review*, Fall, 1982, p. 41.

5. *Marketing and Distribution Strategies of Foreign Products in Japan*, Japan External Trade Organization (JETRO), Tokyo (undated), p. 7.

6. Mitsuaki Shimaguchi and Larry J. Rosenberg, "Demystifying Japanese Distribution," *Columbia Journal of World Business*, Spring, 1979, p. 36.

7. Mitsuaki Shimaguchi and William Lazer, "Japanese Distribution Channels: Invisible Barriers to Market Entry," *MSU Business Topics*, Winter, 1979, Vol. 27, No. 1, pp. 57–58.

13

Retailing In Japan

This chapter will explore the retail structure in Japan. After discussing the types of intermediaries with a retail function in the market and drawing comparisons with the United States, the retail process will be discussed.

THE RETAILING STRUCTURE

The Japanese retailers are specialized along the dimensions of store type and products carried. In terms of types of stores, the primary categories of retailers are department stores, installment sales department stores, general merchandise stores, super-stores (often also referred to as supermarkets), convenience stores, and specialty stores. Within each of these functions, retailers can also be categorized by product specialty such as food, clothing, and household goods.

Department stores are one of the most traditional retail institutions in Japan. Some date back several centuries and many are linked with railroads and railway lines, as stores were typically established at important end terminals. No philosophical conflict arises between running a department store and running a railroad. As one store manager explained, "The railroad is there to serve the consumer as is the department store." This service orientation is especially important. Both employees and customers are constantly reminded of it, and it is symbolized strongly each morning during the opening of the store. During the opening, which is a ceremony that lasts several minutes, the chief officers of each store stand at the doors to welcome the customers with bows. All personnel—whether store employed or supplied by the other channel members—stand in the hallways bowing to the customers and thanking them for their patronage. Merchandise is priced in the medium to high zone, with more and more luxury products being offered. Frequently, tenants within the buildings offer specialty goods. These tenants pay either rent and a commission on their sales or a commission only to the department stores.

Installment sales department stores are similar to their namesakes described above, except for the fact that most purchases there are handled on an installment plan, which many customers find attractive.

General merchandise stores and supermarkets are similar to each other in terms of merchandise, but they differ in size. Both handle a wide range of merchandise and initially competed on the basis of price. Increasingly, however, their main products have been traded up, and they frequently offer luxury items. Supermarkets also tend to carry a substantial variety of food products.

Specialty stores that concentrate on a deep product mix can be differentiated primarily by their product focus. One group offers luxurious items in great assortment, while another focuses on volume products and competes mainly on the basis of price.

Finally, convenience stores comprise the vast majority of Japanese retailers. They are mainly small retail shops that cater to a very limited customer area. These small retailers are able to compete with larger stores due to their lower cost structure. Estimates are that in 1974 retailers with less than ten employees operated with a cost factor of 21.6 percent of sales volume, while retailers with more than 100 employees needed a cost factor of 39.6 percent of sales. This ratio changes, however, if all calculatory costs (for example, salaries of the owners) are included for smaller retailers.[1]

TABLE 13.1. Retailers in Japan

Area of Concentration	No. of Establishments	Percentage
Tokyo	159,568	9.53
Osaka	123,316	7.37
Aichi	84,529	5.05
Hyogo	73,568	4.40
Kanagawa	72,747	4.35
Fukuoka	66,371	3.97
Hokkaido	65,367	3.91
Saitama	59,305	3.51
Shizuoka	52,048	3.11
Chiba	51,181	3.05
Hiroshima	39,794	2.38
Others	825,617	49.34
Total	1,673,411	100.00

Source: *Statistics of Commerce*, Ministry of International Trade and Industry, 1979.

In 1979 Japan had a total of 1.673 million retail establishments. (Table 13.1 provides a breakdown of retailers by area of concentration.) While there is an intensity of retailers in the areas of Tokyo and Osaka, their concentration is substantially less than that of the wholesalers. As shown previously, Tokyo contains over 17.7 percent of all wholesalers, but only 9.5 percent of all retailers. Also, almost 50 percent of all retailers are outside the major areas of concentration, whereas this was the case for only 38 percent of the wholesalers. This suggests that retailers are widely dispersed in Japan and often fulfill their function by being in quite remote areas.

A comparison between the United States and Japanese retail structure is shown in Table 13.2. Japan has only 10 percent fewer retailers than the United States, even though the United States is much larger geographically. Japanese retailers also have substantially fewer employees: 3.6 employees as compared to an average of 6.9 employees per retailer in the United States. Total annual sales of the Japanese retail sector are less than half those of U.S. retailers. Similarly, annual sales per Japanese retailer are only half of the annual sales of U.S. retailers. Also, the population

TABLE 13.2. A Comparison between the Japanese
and the U.S. Retail Structure

	Japan	United States	
	1979	1977	1979
Number of retailers (thousands)	1,673	1,855	—
Number of employees (thousands)	5,960	12,740	13,726
Total annual sales ($ billion)	330	725	1,076
Annual sales per retailer ($ thousands)	197	391	—
Population per retailer	69	122	—
Number of employees per retailer	3.6	6.9	—

Sources: For Japan data: Statistics of Commerce, Ministry of International Trade and Industry, 1979. For U.S. data: Statistical Abstract of the U.S., 1984 Ed. (1977 latest fully available data), U.S. Department of Commerce, Washington, D.C., 1984.

served per retailer is substantially less when compared to the United States.

Table 13.3 supplies additional data on the size of Japanese retailers. As can be seen, more than 85 percent of retailers have fewer than four employees. Large-sized retailers with 30 employees and over comprise only 0.8 percent of the total.

Table 13.4 provides a breakdown of retail industry sales in Japan by types of stores. Total industry sales have grown phenomenally during the past decades, with annual growth averaging 17.6 percent. The rate of growth, however, has slowed down significantly during the past few years. Department stores, though small in number, currently have a substantial market share. This market share, however, has been shrinking since 1974. In comparison to the United States the largest Japanese department store chains are dwarfed by the sales volume of their U.S. counterparts. Only two Japanese retailers, Daiei and Ito-Yokado, would enter a listing of the 20 largest U.S. retailers.[2] Self-service stores have enjoyed the most rapid real growth. In 1979 they had a market share of almost 15 percent, part of which appears to be derived by attracting sales previously handled by department stores. Other retail stores have declined constantly in terms of their market share, although they have managed to participate in the general growth of retail industry sales.

TABLE 13.3. The Size of Japanese Retailers in 1979

Number of Employees	Number of Establishments	Percentage
Small-sized (1-4)	1,423,409	85.1
Medium-sized (5-29)	236,089	14.1
Large-sized (30 and over)	13,913	0.8

Source: *Statistics of Commerce, Ministry of International Trade and Industry, 1979.*

As far as imported consumer products are concerned, department stores and superstores are the primary carriers. Of total sales volume by these types of stores, imports typically account for 10 to 20 percent.[3] Since imports are frequently of high value, their share of total merchandise volume is substantially lower. Retailers other than department stores and superstores sell much less imported merchandise.

Large retailers typically have 50 percent retail margins, resulting in a mark-up of 100 percent. The average retailer receives 46 percent of its merchandise from primary wholesalers, 2 percent from secondary wholesalers, 35 percent from tertiary wholesalers, and 17 percent direct from manufacturers abroad.[4] While small retailers must obtain their goods from wholesalers, large retailers are sometimes able to buy directly from manufacturers.

In the case of imports, large retailers have two basic options: direct and indirect imports. The typical cost of direct importation is 35 to 45 percent of product price, which includes freight, insurance, customs clearance, inland transportation, and import duties. Using the 50 percent retail margin figure will therefore result in a store price of 250 to 290 percent of manufacturer's price. In the case of indirect imports through trading houses or agents, this percentage is generally higher, often reaching 350 percent of the foreign manufactuing price. Due to the resulting high prices, retailers are often faced with the need to either accept lower margins or abandon the importation of products. As a consequence, larger retailers tend more and more to purchase imports directly, and sometimes form their own importing group. One such group is the Allied Import Co., which was formed by Jusco, Uny, Izumiya, and Chujitsuya in 1979 for the purpose of joint

TABLE 13.4. Retail Sales Industry in Japan (U.S. $ billion)

Fiscal Year	Retail Total	Growth Rate (percent)	Department Stores		Self-Service Stores		Other Retail Stores	
1966	47.9	—	4.7	(9.76)*	2.6	(5.44)*	40.6	(84.80)*
1968	74.0	54.5	6.3	(8.47)	4.6	(6.23)	63.1	(85.30)
1970	97.6	31.9	8.9	(9.12)	7.2	(7.41)	81.5	(83.47)
1972	126.9	29.9	12.0	(9.43)	11.0	(8.65)	103.9	(81.92)
1974	180.7	42.4	18.2	(10.07)	19.1	(10.56)	143.4	(79.37)
1976	251.3	39.0	21.9	(8.69)	30.3	(12.05)	199.1	(79.26)
1979	330.0	31.3	26.7	(8.10)	49.0	(14.86)	254.3	(77.04)

*Figures in parentheses indicate market share

Source: Dodwell Marketing Consultants, The Structure of Japanese Retail Distribution Industry 1981/1982, Tokyo, 1981, p. 17.

importation of clothing, houseware goods, leisure goods, and foodstuffs.

Figures 13.1 and 13.2 provide examples of the benefits of direct versus indirect imports for a retail importing group. As can be seen, in both instances the flow of merchandise through various wholesaling levels has been reduced to comprise only a company internal wholesaler or distribution center. As a result, the importer has achieved savings of 25 percent and 17 percent, respectively. Using such shorter channels heightens the potential for imports. While the benefits of shorter channels apply equally well to domestic products, they are more difficult to implement since, other than for newly imported products where distribution channels are newly created for the retailer, domestic products are produced by established manufacturers who already have ties with channel members.

THE RETAILING PROCESS

Retailers in Japan are very demanding of manufacturers and wholesalers. As was mentioned previously, they expect returns of merchandise to be fully accepted even if there is no reason for the return other than the lack of sales capability. As a result, returns from retailers to wholesalers and subsequently to manufacturers are two to five times that in the United States. Retailers also expect substantial amounts of financing and frequent delivery of products from wholesalers and manufacturers. For example, food retailers expect delivery times for vegetables from cutting to store to be less than six hours.

However, retailers also offer substantial services to their clientele, and frequently take great pains to build a relationship with their customers. For example, one chain suggests to its customers that, once a week, all contents of the refrigerator should be replaced. Monday has been chosen by the store as the official replacement day on which discounts are offered. The store claims that if restocking is always done on Mondays, a family can save up to 30,000 yen (U.S. $133) per year. Some stores suggest eating habits for holiday periods or offer special weekend services. Others have a special awareness of family life.

A. Conventional Route

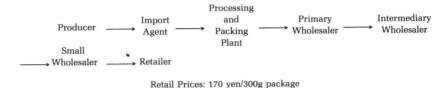

Retail Prices: 170 yen/300g package

B. Restructured Route

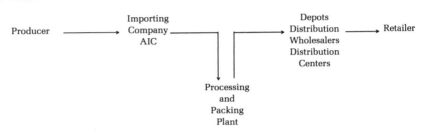

Savings: 25%   Retail price: 128 yen/300g package

FIGURE 13.1.   Example of Import Distribution Alternatives—
Distribution Route of Italian Spaghetti and Macaroni
   Source: Allied Import Company.

For example, since husbands are at home on weekends, heavy items that husbands usually carry and products that husbands like to eat are discounted on weekends. One unique Japanese custom is that retailers frequently organize consumers into purchasing clubs. Consumers register with the retailer as members and their purchases are recorded. This mechanism of full cooperation between retailers and consumer permits the retailer to keep a record of the sales and to award a bonus to consumers who purchase given quantities during the year.

   Retailers, particularly the larger ones, take pride in offering integrated selling systems. For example, sports sections within department stores do not sell sports products in a pedestrian fashion. Constantly rolling video films, often supplied by the manufacturer, demonstrate equipment use on the shopping

A. Conventional Route

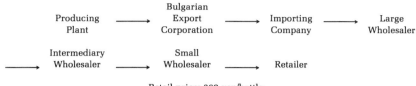

Retail price: 360 yen/bottle

B. Restructured Route

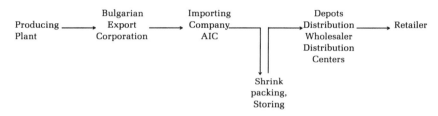

Savings: 17%   Retail price: 300 yen/bottle

FIGURE 13.2.   Example of Import Distribution Alternatives—
Distribution Route of Bulgarian Strawberry Jam
   Source: Allied Import Company.

floor. Some stores even have a sports studio for their own video programming. Sports events are also transmitted and tapes of international tournaments are offered to customers. Stores often hire well-known former athletes as sales personnel who can provide customers not only with advice, but also with photographic opportunities and autographs.

   Small retailers appeal to the convenience needs of consumers. Since until recently Japan's per capita income was too low to permit buying large quantities at one time, and since most Japanese households lack storage space and housewives prefer to shop several times a week in neighborhood stores, convenience often plays a major role. Besides the sociability of these shops, their owners perform special and personal services that supermarkets or department stores do not.[5] While the per capita income situation has changed, small retailer are still important. Since customers and retailers are frequently in locations that suffer from poor automobile access, most customers come by train, on foot, or on bicycle, and therefore can purchase and carry only limited quantities.

Given all the support retailers receive from other channel members and their close interaction with their customers, one would expect the retail business to be quite easy. However, this perception would be misleading. Retailing in Japan is an extremely competitive business, mainly due to the fact that the Japanese are among the world's most demanding customers. Their demands translate into exceedingly high requirements in terms of product freshness and in terms of a precise product-need fit. Perfect products are imperative. For example, pinstriped suits on which the stripes do not carry over perfectly from the shoulder to the front portion of the jacket are unacceptable to most consumers. Due to the competition, consumers have very clear and defined ideas about the height, size, tastes, color, and packaging of merchandise. All these requirements, of course, do not exclude the factor of price competition. However, in a trade-off situation, Japanese consumers are able to value the delivery of service and accept its higher cost. As a result, many retailers are competing fiercely in the area of sales service. Department store personnel, for example, will carefully check every part of a product a customer has selected before packaging it. If slight defects are found, the product will not be sold even if the customer is willing to take it, since long-range unhappiness could result. Great attention also is paid to packaging and wrapping, particularly during gift-giving seasons. As a result, the cost of packaging may sometimes exceed the value of the product sold.

Retailers, being very aware of the level of competition in their field, attempt to get even closer to their customers. Retail stores frequently organize fairs that highlight specific products. Food retailers, which are still the mainstay of retailing due to Japanese dietary habits, try to communicate their customers' needs and demands by working closely with their farm products suppliers. Sometimes this cooperation goes as far as retailers suggesting different growing methods for farmers.

As a result of all the demands placed upon them, retailers expect at least the same, if not even more, service support for imported products than is obtained for domestic merchandise.

However, if such support is given, products can be marketed effectively. The case of Rosenthal porcelain, imported from West Germany, may serve as an example here. Rosenthal products, consisting mainly of porcelain, glass, and figurines, are very successful in Japan. Interestingly enough, these products are bought by customers more for gift-giving purposes than for personal use. The Rosenthal product mix in Japan is quite different from the mix in other countries. The main emphasis is on ornaments and tea items that can be given as gifts, and not on plates as in the United States. In order to be aware of what items are and could be in major demand and to adjust its production strategy accordingly, Rosenthal constantly conducts marketing research in Japan. Over the past 20 years the firm has developed a close relationship with Japanese retailers and frequently invites store personnel to visit the factories in Germany. In Japan itself, the company provides precise instruction for product display, even coordinating the colors within the displays. The firm has stationed employees permanently in Japan whose sole purpose is to work closely with retailers and distributors. Due to this very active representation, retailers can expect at least weekly contact with Rosenthal. In addition, the German company has developed a training program for Japanese retailers. Every year Japanese store employees go to the Rosenthal factory in Germany to learn about customer counseling. These trips, for which all expenses are paid by Rosenthal, last ten days. Retailers are pleased with all that support and are eager to carry Rosenthal products, particularly since they offer comfortable profit margins.

While the support service activities offered by Rosenthal are unique even for Japan, they highlight the need for importers to display great sensitivity to product-adaptation requirements since Japanese customers show little willingness to compromise their precise needs. However, an unwillingness to adapt products to market needs, particularly on the part of U.S. manufacturers, often results in great desperation on the part of actual and potential Japanese importers.

The unwillingness of U.S. manufacturers to adapt to foreign market requirements has perhaps become most widely known internationally by the refusal to change the side of the steering wheel for cars exported to Japan. The same problem, however, also exists for smaller manufacturers. Executives of one Japanese department store, for example, produced eight years of correspondence with U.S. furniture manufacturers. Apart from quality issues, these letters dealt mainly with the need for furniture to be smaller for the Japanese market. However, despite substantial prodding and advice, this particular retailer was not able to locate a single U.S. furniture manufacturer who was willing to reduce the size of the standard furniture. As a result, the store decided to purchase British goods from a manufacturer who was more willing to make such changes. Even though such changes may mean, particularly at the beginning of a business relationship, that economies of scale in production have to be foregone, they are necessary in order to be successful.

Retailers, however, realize that such shifts in production may result in substantial costs. They are fully willing to give new merchandise a chance by sticking with it for a prolonged period of time. Even if demand and profitability are low, they will devote substantial portions of display space to products if they feel that the manufacturer and the channel members are willing to give the product long-range support and if they believe in the product's eventual success. It is not unheard of that retailers support products with no or minimal profit for several years in order to gradually introduce them to the public.

In conclusion, it can be said that the Japanese retail process is characterized by an extremely high service orientation, expectations for long-range commitments, the need for close cooperation with the channel members, and substantial financing requirements.

NOTES

1. Helmut Laumer, *Die Warendistribution in Japan*, Institut Fuer Asienkunde, Hamburg, 1979, p. 88.

2. *Investors Guide 1983*, Ito-Yokado Co., Ltd., Tokyo, 1983, p. 27.

3. *Retailing in the Japanese Consumer Market*, JETRO Marketing Series 5, Tokyo, 1979, pp. 42–43.

4. Laumer, op. cit., p. 33.

5. Mitsuaki Shimaguchi and Larry J. Rosenberg, "Demystifying Japanese Distribution," *Columbia Journal of World Business*, Spring, 1979, p. 35.

14

Changes Coming About

The preceding chapters provided an overview of the Japanese distribution system. However, even though the system is a result of tradition, it contains an inherent dynamism that results in numerous changes. Frequently these changes are not recognized. From the outside, the Japanese distribution system is often perceived today as it was 20 years ago. As is true with most allegations and suspicions, many assumptions about this system have remained in force even long after their basis is gone. This is not to say that the system has been completely supplanted by something new, but rather that changes have come that have been little noticed, but that indicate and to some extent have already resulted in major shifts in the functions, structure, and processes of the system. These changes have come about not for the purpose of change per se, but as a reaction to changing realities. Perhaps these changes are best characterized by Keiichi Konaga, the director of the Industrial Policy Bureau of the Ministry of Trade and Industry: "It remains to be seen whether the quantitative maturation of the Japanese economy, following two rounds of sharp oil price increases, shall lead to a better life for the consumer and produce a sense of fulfillment among the Japanese people. As consumer needs diversify with emphasis on quality rather than on quantity, it becomes increasingly important for the distribution industry to meet these needs."[1]

CHANGES IN THE JAPANESE WHOLESALING SECTOR

Many changes are occurring today in the Japanese wholesaling structure. However, in typical Japanese fashion, these changes do not come about with fanfare—they take place in a quiet and subtle way. Table 14.1 provides information about recent trends in the wholesale industry with a particular focus on changes in the number of establishments, number of employees, and annual sales over the years. The data show that the wholesaling sector grew rapidly, particularly in terms of sales volume, up to 1974, when the two-year increase in annual sales reached 62 percent. However, during the same two-year period the wholesale index in Japan also increased sharply. At the same time, the number of establishments and employees grew substantially, but at a much lower rate. In the past few year, however, the rate of growth has slowed significantly. On an annualized basis, the number of establishments grew by only 2.8 percent, the number of employees by only 1.6 percent, and the sale volume by 8.3 percent.

These changes were to a large extent initiated during the period of the oil shock. Wholesalers frequently demanded large price hikes from their customers. While most customers were forced to accept these increases, many larger retailers decided it would be more advantageous in the long run to go directly to the manufacturers instead. Also, by building their own distribution centers, these retailers were able to rely less on wholesalers.

As a result of these developments, the Japanese proverb "You can't fight the tonya" has lost much of its veracity today. The power of wholesalers as channel members is said to be on the decline. Concurrently, the social status of wholesaling has decreased. This fact translates directly into personnel capabilities, since young people now prefer joining manufacturers or retailers rather than wholesaling firms.

Increased Integration

The wholesaling sector, however, does not intend to give up its preeminent position without a fight. Increasingly, the sector is marked by both vertical and horizontal integration activities.[2] One trend that can be observed is the formation of manufacturer-wholesalers. These are firms that produce some merchandise, but subcontract the major part of their production.

TABLE 14.1. Selected Trends in the Japanese Wholesale Industry: 1970–79

Year	Number of Establishments	Percentage Change	Number of Employees (in 1000s)	Percentage Change	Annual Sales Volume (U.S. $ mill)	Percentage Change
1970	255,974	—	2,861	—	366.5	—
1972	259,163	1.2	3,008	5.1	443.1	21.0
1974	292,155	12.7	3,290	9.4	718.3	62.1
1976	340,249	16.5	3,513	6.7	922.5	28.4
1979	368,686	8.3	3,688	6.0	1,151.0	24.8

*In 1973 and 1974, the wholesale price index increased by 15.9 percent and 31.4 percent respectively (source: *International Statistics*, 1982).

Source: *Commercial Census*, Ministry of International Trade and Industry, 1981.

This is particularly the case in the men's and women's apparel industry, where manufacturers absorb the wholesalers. In some instances, however, wholesalers have absorbed smaller manufacturers and have begun to integrate the retailing sector. Larger wholesalers also consolidate their activities with those of the secondary or tertiary partners in order to retain their market position. These integrated firms can pose problems for importers of merchandise, since a wholesaler is more likely to buy from its manufacturing firm than from a foreign firm. Even if imported products are purchased, their distribution may be limited if the Japanese manufacturing arm of the wholesaler begins to produce a competing product. By the same token, wholesalers that grow larger and stronger through integration are able to establish more international linkages and import more than smaller wholesalers.

However, this integration is not all-pervasive. There are still many manufacturers who produce small-lot merchandise for which wholesalers are necessary. Channel members at the manufacturing and the retailing level are often still heavily dependent on wholesaler financing. Also, many manufacturers, even if they could deliver certain goods directly, maintain their relationships with wholesalers for all transactions in order not to lose the small retailers they could not service if direct distribution were to be introduced and ties with wholesalers severed.

New Distribution Systems

Because of and in addition to these structural changes, the wholesaling process is also undergoing significant shifts. The migration to cities has resulted in greater urban congestion. Wholesalers and distributors located in the middle of urban centers face shortages of space and transportation problems. Also, a higher standard of living and a greater variety of goods place more demands on wholesalers. In addition, small wholesalers achieve less and less return on investment because they are often heavily involved in the financing of channel members and can sell only to small retailers.

Recognizing the problems of the wholesaling sector, the Japanese government in the late 1960s began to legislate distribution improvements. An area in which these improvements gradually came to bear is the one of distribution zones, which result from the formation of government-sponsored joint ventures between small firms, large warehouse companies, and terminals for the purpose of creating more modern storage and warehouse facilities. The newly formed centers contain distribution warehouses, display space, office buildings, and space for parking. High warehouse buildings with direct truck access offer efficient space utilization. Warehousing space is fully climatized and largely automated. The administration of such centers also provides for maintenance, security, and common facilities such as cafeterias. As a result, tenants need to worry only about their own business. This specialization has a positive impact on firms. One company, for example, which previously needed to maintain 20 depots in Tokyo with a total of 400 employees, now reports occupying only one floor in a warehouse and working with 80 employees.

Apart from these government activities, manufacturers themselves are forming distribution centers and joining forces with other manufacturing firms to provide a wide assortment of products. Some manufacturers who in the past delivered exclusively to wholesalers are now, due to pressures from the retail sector, frequently delivering direct to retailers. While many wholesalers still receive a commission despite the direct flow of goods from manufacturers to retailers, these payments are often the result of old ties. As the older generation dies out, tradition might become less pervasive and such payments may become less frequent.

Changes in Transportation

Another major change is that wholesalers in cities are increasingly unable to provide competitive delivery service. A trend to order-consolidation can be observed, particularly in the newer warehousing zones. More and more transportation companies are being formed exclusively for order-consolidation purposes. In cooperation with wholesalers or alone, such firms can achieve major transport economies. Transportation cost saving average about 30 percent and are sometimes as high as 60 percent. Consolidation is growing rapidly among wholesalers since nonusers are suffering severely from the competitive advantage of the low transportation cost of users. By turning over the delivery function to outside companies, the activities of many wholesalers change substantially. Rather than focusing mainly on delivery, they concentrate on providing financing, break bulk, and assortment services.

Many regional wholesalers are also changing their activities. As many small manufacturers die out because they cannot compete against larger firms, the need for regional wholesalers diminishes, since the large firms often need no financing from small wholesalers. As a result, these wholesalers, rather than sending products from their region to large consumption centers as they have done in the past, begin now to bring in products from these centers for distribution in their region.

New Business Relations

Some of the traditions of the wholesaling process are also undergoing shifts. For example, the time-honored way of establishing ties and then sticking with one's business partners is changing. A reassessment of channels is increasingly done by channel participants, and switches are made if financially necessary.

Such a shift from traditional ways of doing business can perhaps be seen most clearly by looking at the emergence of cash-and-carry wholesalers, who are enjoying substantial rates of growth. Their primary competitive tool is price. These firms aim at those retailers that do not require financing or delivery service. Frequently, their main customers are the very small retailers who come everyday to purchase products for 70,000 yen (U.S. $300) or less. These wholesalers refuse to accept returns from retailers and suggest instead that they discount slow-selling merchandise. No personal linkages are developed and no rebates or bonuses are granted.

In their dealings with manufacturers, these cash-and-carry wholesalers are similarly unconventional. No personal relationship is developed here either. These firms deal with many small manufacturers and select suppliers only on the basis of product and price competitiveness. While this method of doing business results in low prices, such cash-and-carry wholesalers often cannot sell national brand merchandise, since many large and well-known manufacturers are unwilling to sell to them. However, in spite of this handicap, these firms have annual inventory turnovers as high as thirty, while conventional consumer goods wholesalers achieve an average annual inventory turnover of seven. Increasingly, these pioneers are handling their own importing and exporting, and therefore can be valuable allies of a foreign manufacturer.

In sum, the major changes in wholesaling are occurring along the following dimensions:

- An increased focus on competitiveness results in a major emphasis on efficiency
- In order to retain market power, substantial horizontal and vertical integration is taking place
- These changes in structure and process increasingly deemphasize business customs that are the result of traditions
- While many channel members, in spite of changes in activity, still aim to maintain old behaviors, these changes have made room for reorientation of current wholesalers, and the emergence of new types of channel participants
- All present factors indicate a period of transition where time is on the side of the new and efficient.

CHANGES IN THE JAPANESE RETAILING SYSTEM

Even though the structure of channels is the one business activity that, particularly from the macro perspective, is changing most slowly, some trends and shifts can be recognized in the Japanese retailing system. Table 14.2 provides a general overview of selected trends in the Japanese retail industry. As can be seen, in recent years sales, which in the early 1970s had been growing spectacularly, have been increasing at a substantially slower rate. The even lower rate of increase in the number of employees and the number of establishments indicates that productivity increases

TABLE 14.2. Selected Trends in the Japanese Retail Industry

Year	Total Sales ($ bill.)	Pct. Change	No. of Employees (10,000s)	Pct. Change	Estab. per 1000 pop.	Pct. Change
1968	74	—	465	—	14.1	—
1972	127	72	514	10.5	13.9	(1.4)
1976	251	98	558	8.6	14.3	2.9
1979	330	31	596	6.8	14.4	0.7
1982*	422	28	638	7.0	14.6	1.4

*Preliminary.
Source: Census of Commerce, Japanese Ministry of International Trade and Industry, 1984.

TABLE 14.3. Trends in Retail Store Size

	1968	1972	1976	1979	1983*
Number of establishments (10,000 stores)	143.2	149.6	161.4	167.4	172.2
Sales floor area (10,000 sq. meters)	4,758	6,111	7,497	8,574	9,678
Sales floor area/store (m²)	34.2	46.6	48.8	54.1	59.7

*Preliminary.
Source: Census of Commerce, Japanese Ministry of International Trade and Industry, 1984.

are still high. In terms of establishments relative to the population, one can see that while from 1968 to 1972 a drop occurred, this trend has been reversed. In the past few years, the number of retail establishments as a proportion of the population has been going up at an increasing rate.

Table 14.3 provides more information regarding trends in retail store size. From 1968 to 1982 the number of retail establishments increased by 20 percent. During the same time, the sales floor area increased by 100 percent. This shows that stores have grown in size and that this growth has rested primarily with the larger stores. This observation is confirmed when one scrutinizes the average sales floor area per store. From an average size of 34.2 square meters in 1968, store size rose in 1982 to an average of 59.7 square meters. However, within this general trend, some changes have taken place in the more recent past. The number of establishments, which from 1968 to 1972 had grown on an annualized basis by 1.4 percent, grew only 1 percent per year from 1979 to 1982. The decline has been more dramatic for the sales floor space, where an overall annual growth rate of 7.4 percent dropped to a growth rate of 4.3 percent during the 1979 to 1982 period. It appears, therefore, that the strong push in the growth of large stores has diminished in recent years.

The Big Store Law

This development, of course, is no accident. While some trace it back to changes in consumer behavior and demands, others claim that the primary reason for this development lies with the Large-Scale Retail Store Law. This legislation has its roots in the 1956 Department Store Law, which was passed to protect small- and medium-sized retailers from department stores. The law, which regulated the opening of department stores and increases in their size, applied to stores that had a selling area of over 1,500 square meters. In the 11 largest cities of Japan, it applied only to stores with a selling area of over 3,000 square meters. It provided for a council of consumers, academics, representatives of small- and medium-sized stores, and representatives from local department stores under the aegis of the local Chamber of Commerce to evaluate all plans for new stores. Due to various justified and unjustified fears, many of these councils turned out to be an onerous burden for companies planning to open department stores. In order to circumvent the law, stores were opened with slightly less than 1,500 square meters' selling space, and some chains formed groups of companies that would purchase a building and open "different" stores on each floor, with each floor being slightly less than 1,500 meters. Since the law applied to stores occupying buildings with a total space of over 10,000 square meters or a total selling space over 6,000 square meters, usually four "different" stores were found in any one building.

Due to its circumvention, in March 1974 the Large-Scale Retail Store Law was passed, with the expressed interest of promoting the development of a "balanced" retail industry. The law attempted to reconcile the interests of large retail stores with the interest of smaller retailers in the same locality, while at the same time giving due consideration to the interests of consumers. Companies planning to open stores with a sales floor space of over 1,500 meters are now required to notify the Ministry of International Trade and Industry of their plans. In addition, no more subdivision of buildings was possible. Local area councils known as Commercial Activities Adjustments Boards were now in charge of deciding the restrictions to be placed on any new large stores with regard to sales floor space, closing hours, the proposed opening date, and the number of store holidays per month.

In 1979 the Large-Scale Retail Store Law was amended to apply to stores with sales floor space exceeding 500 square meters. While the procedures of this amendment were generally the same as with the previous law, the newly covered smaller stores were required to notify the local prefectural government rather than MITI. This in turn resulted in some local prefectures and city councils passing additional ordinances that restrict the establishment of stores with a size of 300 or even 200 square meters.

All these regulations require registration and notification, but not approval by MITI. On the surface, therefore, they appear to have a minor impact on the further development of larger stores. This, however, is not the case. MITI will only accept a notification if the applicant can show unanimous consent from the local boards. Since these boards or councils are composed of a wide variety of individuals in order to be better sounding boards for MITI, it is difficult for any applicant to obtain such consent. As a result, the application process becomes excessively time-consuming and costly, particularly since the requirements placed on stores continue to become more restrictive. Also, when the application process is passed, store maintenance can become expensive and sometimes even economically unfeasible, due to, for example, closing hour restrictions that were imposed to provide smaller retailers with a better competitive chance. Since the big store law now covers virtually all the self-service stores except the smaller convenience stores, it has quite a negative effect on the opening of new, larger-sized stores.

The law exists, of course, in recognition of the major role the small-scale retail sector plays in the Japanese economy. Reorganization of such a sector is likely to cause social and political tensions. Larger stores try to reduce these by coopting their smaller brethren through franchising or taking them in as tenants into their larger stores. Given the small retailer's desire to be completely independent, however, this is not always possible.

The Evolution of Chain Stores

Small retailers are not about to disappear, and many of them will continue to survive and prosper. MITI's industrial policy bureau sees the future for smaller retailers mainly in the organization of small stores into voluntary and franchised store chains. MITI is apparently willing to lend its support to such a development, since one of its officials stated that "the organization of small retailers is . . . important as they represent the greater part of the Japanese retail industry."[3]

The formation of such chains represents another fundamental shift in the retail channel structure. More and more chains have come about, particularly in the convenience store sector. Since 1977 this sector has experienced an annual average growth rate of 32 percent. Total sales of the 33 leading chain stores from 1982 amounted to approximately U.S. $3.4 billion.[4]

These stores are typically located in residential areas, carry only goods needed daily, and are open long hours. In most instances, these stores are part of chains and are owned by an individual on a franchise or volunteer basis. The chain management provides owners with help and training in the areas of management techniques and stocking policies. The largest convenience store chain in Japan is 7–11. By the end of February 1984, it had 2000 stores with 350 to 400 new outlets expected to open every year. Despite the small size of the individual store, the chain as a whole posted sales of $24 million for Coca-Cola, $29 million for instant Chinese noodles, and $63 million for magazines, each boasting the largest sales ever achieved by a single corporation. As for the merchandise on display at the store, 1,800 items out of 3,000 to 3,500 have been replaced by different merchandise in the past half year in response to consumer needs.[5] Another similarly large and growing voluntary chain is Kei-Mart, whose management also works with sophisticated technology to meet consumer needs. It has just introduced the voluntary chain information system (VOIS), which provides selling information from all its stores and permits for purchasing of 68 percent of the merchandise by headquarters.

Emergence of Nonstore Retailing

Another area of substantial structural change is that of nonstore retailing. Mail order firms are increasing their activities substantially. Although these nonstore retailers still face problems in the area of designing an effective physical distribution system and difficulties in overcoming the high initial costs of media fees and catalog production, some firms reportedly are already profitable. Even though they represent only a small percentage of retail industry sales, mail order firms are beginning to improve their performance.

Experiments are also carried out with new types of distribution channels with the support of the Ministry of International Trade and Industry. A major one is the development of two-way interactive cable television by HI-OVIS. This project, which was initiated in 1976 and is currently in its Phase II, permits the two-way transmission of both voice and picture. It allows individuals to request the showing of specific videotapes on their television sets. In addition to offering programs in areas such as instruction, physical fitness, and entertainment, HI-OVIS experiments with providing retail functions. Large companies are given time slots to explain products and to interact with viewers. A tele-shopping program is offered in which viewers can examine merchandise and find out about prices. While this live program is enjoyed by the viewers, it has not been enthusiastically received by retailers and has not yet resolved the settlement problem—that is, how do customers pay for their orders? On-line settlement, however, was planned to be instituted in late 1984.

Currently, HI-OVIS is still in an experimental stage. It is faced with great challenges in the areas of initial investment cost, consumer resistance to costly system purchases, and transmission technology constraints. At the same time, current audience acceptance is high, and some railroad companies, which in times past were the original founders of the department stores, have indicated an interest in investment possibilities.

Adjustments to Changes
in Consumer Behavior

In spite of the claims by some researchers that "the facts appear to be that little distributive change has occurred [in Japan] and that improvement in this sector will take a great deal of time,"[6] we see the retailing process as undergoing substantial shifts. These are primarily the result of changing consumer behavior. Due to changes in income levels and the desire for more originality, Japanese consumer needs have diversified over the years. Many consumers have already satisfied most of their demand for physical goods and have filled the available space in their homes. Increasingly, consumer demand is focusing on nonproduct areas, as can be seen in the gradual trend in consumer spending patterns shown in Table 14.4. An increasing proportion of expenditures goes toward services, while the product portion of consumer expenditures is decreasing. As a result, the mission of larger retailers is changing. Rather than being simple sellers of products, they have become marketers of culture. Japanese consumers have also become much more sensitized to prices due to the inflation following the oil shock and consumer education campaigns. Increasingly, consumers find large stores' lower prices appealing and prefer to rely on brand names rather than on retail personnel advice.[7] Consumers have also become more accepting of the self-service concept, and display a clear trend toward the demand of convenience. Other trends are:

- A shorter work week, which permits more time for leisure activities such as sports and pleasure trips
- A renewed orientation toward crafts
- Sharp increase in consumer acceptance of financing

TABLE 14.4. Trends in Distribution of Consumer Spending
(per household as percentage of total expenditures)

	Goods	Services	Other
1965	55.4	32.7	11.9
1970	53.0	34.8	12.2
1975	50.7	37.1	12.2
1980	46.5	39.3	14.2
1981	46.1	39.0	14.9
1982	45.2	39.9	14.9

Source: *Investors Guide 1983*, Ito-Yokado Co., Ltd. p. 20.

- Renewed focus on cultural events—people again taking courses in literature, flower arranging, and calligraphy but do so side-by-side with computer courses[8]
- A fashion orientation within households that focuses not just on clothes, but also on furniture and eating utensils
- An increase in disposable income and a willingness to spend, particularly since empty-nest housewives enter the labor market in order for the household to be able to afford luxury services
- An increased focus on spiritual enrichment rather than on products only

Concurrent with those developments in consumer behavior, retailers are also seeing changes in employee attitudes. While the willingness to serve is still extremely high, some gradations have become visible. For example, in the department store opening ceremonies, younger employees can be observed to bow not quite as long and not quite as deep as the older ones. Employees are increasingly interested in job diversity and leisure time and hobby activities. This fact is reflected in a new flexible job program initiated by the Seibu Group, a program that is unique by Japanese standards. Beginning in September 1984 the Seibu Group, which comprises 92 companies and employs nearly 70,000 people, offered its workers the opportunity to divide their five-day work week between two jobs, to work on the side on their days off, or to change jobs without losing their seniority—as long as these shifts are made within the group.[9]

More and more retailers, particularly the larger ones, are emphasizing the delivery of services. Frequently one can hear

Japanese executives refer to their stores as culture centers. Services such as travel advice, beauty shops, health programs, real estate, insurance, and evening courses are becoming increasingly part of the new product offering of such stores. Also added are children's play areas and entertainment centers.

Large retailers wish to offer a shopping experience to their consumers, and try to do so by providing luxury products, luxury services, and a luxurious environment. This increases the pressure to offer diversity of products and services. Large retailers also attempt to give themes to their product offerings by regularly holding fairs that introduce or highlight specific product categories for a limited time.

Smaller retailers, in turn, see their main competitive niche in the area of convenience and in providing fresh products. In doing so, they are able to preserve a competitive advantage when compared to larger retailers, who cannot be as fully responsive in their delivery.

Improvements in Distribution Information

A revolution is occurring in the information-processing area within the distribution system. Changes here are only the beginning of things to come. As a MITI representative noted: "The distribution industry is being increasingly required to more effectively meet consumer needs in a maturing industrial society. It must serve not only as a pipeline through which goods flow from producers to consumers, but also as a relay point allowing information to flow between the two. The information function of the distribution industry is expected to increase as the advanced information society develops. In other words, the importance of the distribution industry as a relay point for the flow of producer-consumer information will increase as the Japanese economy matures and handles more information."[10] The progress of this information revolution is apparent when one sees that the distribution industry currently accounts for 43 percent of computers used in all industries in Japan.[11]

These changes are perhaps most visible with the installation of POS (Point of Sale) systems by retailers. This computerized cash register system collects information on all the items sold in the store and is used for research, merchandising, and planning purposes. By encouraging consumers to use store credit cards, which are encoded with socioeconomic customer data, the POS system can identify segments that purchase certain products, preferred size of product package, and the time of day products are purchased. Other than in the United States, privacy laws do not restrict such information flows.

Additional uses of the POS system are for shopping basket analysis, customer traffic analysis, and merchandise layout experimentation. The system also permits more precise demand forecasting and inventory planning, cash register error reduction, and better personnel utilization.

The main purpose of the POS system is, however, not to reduce the number of employees. As one Japanese executive noted: "In the U.S. use of software in supermarkets is made because of 'hard' merits such as savings in labor cost. In Japan we focus more on the 'soft' merits of these innovations such as the use of data for decision-making or for consumer satisfaction." Stores using the system have been able to reduce the number of checkout lanes by up to 20 percent; the freed-up employees are now used to foster more direct contact with customers. More service than before is now provided to customers in areas such as information about merchandise location and product usage. Apart from resulting in more informed and, it is hoped, more content customers, stores expect this increased service orientation to ease new product introduction, enhance product differentiation, and perhaps enable an increasing shift in the new product mix toward products with high explanatory needs.

Dramatic technological changes are also occurring in the international retailing sector. For example, Matsuzakaya, a Nagoya department store, has had a long-standing mail order relationship with Quelle, Germany. Customers of Matsuzakaya were able to select Quelle products from a catalog in Japan. Matsuzakaya then checked the availability of such a selection via air mail. Once availability was confirmed, the customer paid and the merchandise was shipped from Germany. In order to cut down on the lagtime between customer selection and receipt of merchandise, Matsuzakaya is in the process of establishing a direct satellite link with Quelle. Customer catalog selections will now be transmitted directly to Quelle via computer terminals located in the stores. After a check for availability via the on-line system, merchandise can be sent off immediately, thus reducing total order lag-time to two weeks.[12]

Improvements in Distribution Technology

Substantial changes in the retail sector are also taking place in physical distribution technology. A prime example is a Tokyo Seiyu store, which is part of the Seibu Group. This prototype store was opened in 1983 as a result of the finding that, in conventional retail stores, 60 percent of employee time was devoted to the transport of merchandise, 20 percent to clerical and administrative work, and only 20 percent to human interaction. The store is designed to demonstrate the fusion of people and science, by having humans deal mainly with creative issues and services, and machines with the picking, holding, and transporting of products. Apart from offering features such as completely automated slicing and packaging of meat products, new systems for building and cleanliness control, and the use of experimental products, the store has completely automated its physical distribution function. Delivery trucks are parked by the driver and the doors are opened. Crates and pallets are automatically unloaded and transported to the store-attached warehouse, where a fully automated storage system is in place. Sales data are collected from the store through the POS system and are fed into the warehouse system, which in turn carries out the picking function in preparation for restocking. After the store closes, merchandise is automatically retrieved from the warehouse and restocked on the store's shelves. Concurrently, replenishment orders are placed with suppliers.

Although the system still suffers from problems with merchandise that is not bar coded or source marked, it is operative and provides valuable information to the parent company. Seibu, in turn, is planning to use the lessons learned from this new technology application to improve its own stores. It is also planning to develop a consulting package for sale of the system to other stores. This development may well mark a new era. As one U.S. executive noted: "Time was when the stream of visitors to supermarkets was one way, from Japan to the U.S. The Seiyu store may signal a change of direction. More Americans may be packing their bags—along with their Japanese-made cameras and tape recorders—and head west across the Pacific. When Horace Greeley said, 'Go West, young man,' he never dreamed of the implications."[13]

NOTES

1. Keiichi Konaga, "Future of Japan's Distribution Industry," *Densu Japan Marketing Advertising*, Spring, 1984, p. 1.

2. William Lazer, Musata Shoji, and Kosaka Hiroshi, "Japanese Marketing: Towards a Better Understanding," *Journal of Marketing*, Spring, 1985, Vol. 49, No. 2, p. 79.

3. Konaga, op. cit., p. 3.

4. "In the Convenience Store Sector, Strategic Management is a Must," *Japan Times*, December, 1983.

5. Sekikawa Hitomi, "Seven-Eleven Japan Develops About 2,000 Stores," Distribution Code Center, The Distribution Systems Research Institute, Mimeo, Tokyo, February 9, 1984, p. 1.

6. Randolph E. Ross, "Understanding the Japanese Distribution System: An Explanatory Framework," *European Journal of Marketing*, Vol. 17, No. 1, 1983, p. 12.

7. Mitsuaki Shimaguchi and Larry J. Rosenberg, "Demystifying Japanese Distribution," *Columbia Journal of World Business*, Spring, 1979, p. 35.

8. "Softnomics: The Service Oriented Economy of Japan," *JETRO*, No. 35, Tokyo, 1985, p. 2.

9. "Seibu Considering Flexible Job Program," *Japan Times*, March 10, 1984, p. 2.

10. Konaga, op. cit., p. 1.

11. Ibid., p. 2.

12. Kiodo News Release, Tokyo, March, 1984.

13. Robert O'Neill, "Go West Young Man—To Japan?" *Progressive Grocer*, January, 1984, p. 10.

15

Toward A Level Playing Field: Conclusions And Perspectives

The Japanese distribution system is undergoing substantial change as a reflection of changes in the society at large. Business institutions are faced with major shifts in demand, and the increasing unwillingness on the part of consumers to pay unnecessarily high prices. The current Japanese business system serves its market and, in most instances, serves it well. But where the system is inefficient, changes are now taking place.

These developments bode well for foreign businesses waiting to break into the Japanese market. However, it must be understood that most of the market shifts taking place now neither result from, nor are they amenable to, substantial government intervention. Rather they are the outcome of societal change which comes about by consensus. Such change by consensus is always likely to be gradual and may result in institutional configurations in which process outpaces structure and people work without function.

Thus, it is important to recognize the human element of the Japanese business system and the social repercussions of change. The system will not adjust on the basis of business economics alone, but rather on the basis of societal economics.

Despite some need to allow the changes in the Japanese market to occur at their own pace, there are steps that both the Japanese and U.S. public and private sectors need to undertake to enhance U.S.-Japanese economic relations. To aid in this process, several programmatic steps are outlined.

THE JAPANESE PRIVATE SECTOR

The private sector in Japan must finally come to recognize that Japan is facing an import imperative. Much of its prosperity has depended on an international market that is relatively free of constraints, particularly in the case of the United States. However, as trade imbalances between Japan and its major trading partners increase, Japanese access to foreign markets becomes threatened. If Japanese firms expect to retain their international market access, they must demonstrate a willingness to share the benefits they have derived from this access.

Changes in attitude should include a serious consideration of the international trade repercussions of any domestic business decision. For example, it will be of increasing importance to consider sourcing beyond one's *keiretsu* or looking beyond established channel members to give recognition to supply alternatives from abroad. Japanese firms must now consider the necessity of forging new ties and relationships with foreign firms. Foreign suppliers must now enter the picture in order to maintain the benefits of open markets that Japanese business obtained in previous years. The Japanese system is well equipped to handle the additional considerations, especially if proper thought is given to the downward risk incurred if access to the major markets of the world is cut off.

NON-JAPANESE PRIVATE SECTOR

Private sectors of countries desiring to do more business with or in Japan also must undergo some transformation. First and foremost, businesses must recognize the constraints in the Japanese market and develop a willingness and ability to work within those constraints. This will require adjustments in international operation in order to penetrate the market successfully.

Many international business executives still hold a very dim view of the openness of Japanese markets, a view frequently shaped by experiences of the past and often based on the realities of the present. However, with positive developments in the Japanese market now occurring, it is up to the exporting business community to take advantage of these new opportunities.

For example, new chain stores are emerging in Japan. These firms can become valuable allies to importers since they are willing to change the composition of their merchandise offering. In addition, a centralized purchasing function can provide for large-sized orders that would otherwise be difficult to obtain. The centralized distribution employed by many of these chain stores enables their local headquarters to provide many service functions that would be difficult for a foreign supplier to deliver. Since the emergence of these chain stores is relatively recent, this is the time to enter into business relations that can lead to a firm foundation for future interaction.

In a similar vein, exporters should cooperate more fully with Japanese cash-and-carry wholesalers. Due to their lack of allegiance to any specific manufacturer, and their primary focus on price and product, these firms have the potential to become good partners. While the type of clientele attracted by these stores restricts the line of merchandise that can be offered, their continued growth will open up more opportunities. Their main focus will remain on price and product competitiveness, a factor on which foreign firms will need to concentrate.

Similar opportunities for exports also exist with other emerging channel participants. For example, an increase in nonstore retailing has opened up new opportunities in the mail order sector. The willingness of Japanese consumers to accept this direct method of distribution, circumventing existing institutional barriers, may be the greatest single asset to this innovative form of market penetration. Also, the trend toward order-consolidation and the establishment of new transportation companies offer new avenues for cooperation. Most of the new transportation firms are not tied to any specific channel member, but rather aim at providing the most efficient transportation service. In doing so, they are an important complementary ingredient for competitive distribution in Japan.

Exporters should also take advantage of the Japanese information revolution. It is now easier to conduct market research with good, quick results. The improved information flow has also reduced the need for inventory size and, therefore, the level of necessary initial investment.

In order for the exporting firm to benefit from any of these changes, it must improve its own international competitiveness. Firms should increase their focus on product, quality, product consistency, and high service delivery. Furthermore, doing business in Japan does not necessarily imply a departure from all known business rules. Many features of the Japanese business system described herein are also conceptually a part of the U.S. business experience. For example, managers have formal and informal ties among themselves (be it at a club or at the golf course). Channel members also expect service, financing, promotional assistance, and return privileges. It is in the performance and intensity of these activities, however, where the differences between the two markets emerge. Japanese business practices resist change and thus require heavy time, financial, and quality commitments.

Not every firm will be able to afford a long-term commitment of managerial time and financial resources necessary to compete successfully in Japan. For example, even though a firm may know that success for its products mandates the maintenance of a warehouse, the stationing of a service technician, and the establishment of a local presence in Japan, this is not always feasible given limited resources. The decision often boils down to whether there will be enough product sales or sufficient profits to justify the expenditures. Currently, in analyzing cost versus profit potential, many firms decide to forego opportunities.

As an alternative, exporting firms should consider a consortium approach. Firms that are unable to make major commitments out of their own resources may consider joining forces with other companies. Market entry would be much easier if a firm has to support 10 percent of the cost of a warehouse or a service technician. It is here that the mechanism of the export trading company (ETC) can prove to be a major supporting factor for successful business development abroad. Even though this mechanism has not been used much, it offers tremendous potential for cooperation among firms.

JAPAN'S POLICY

The upper echelons of the Japanese policy community have recognized the need to increase Japan's imports. This has led to the implementation of unique trade policies. As was noted by one of the directors of JETRO, "after all, what other nation can you name which has public and private bodies allocating funds to help increase the exports of their trading partners."[1] The new focus on importation requires a move away from the traditional bureaucratic perspective of defense against imports. These bureaucratic attitudes often have been shaped for decades by the grim necessity for exports. In some cases, change can be brought about only by the gradual extinction of old bureaucratic warhorses.

Japanese policy must reflect an understanding of the interlinkage between trade and foreign relations. One hopeful note is provided in a recent MITI document, which states that "it is important to expand the import of manufactured goods [into Japan], not only because greater access to foreign goods will help raise the living standard in Japan, but also because increased purchases will help improve the nation's foreign relations."[2]

In carrying out this mission, Japan's public sector must address both reality and perception. A change in the reality of the Japanese marketplace requires the understanding that there are indeed obstacles to the importation of foreign products, and that reducing these obstacles would be beneficial to Japan. For example, the current restriction on department store growth inhibits foreign consumer products by limiting the availability of potential outlets. Even though these restrictive measures are being implemented mainly for domestic Japanese policy reasons rather than for the purposes of restricting the importation of foreign products, international repercussions are severe.

Many other policy considerations that are currently thought of as being strictly domestic also have international implications. For example, pressure blocs emanating from the tobacco and the citrus sectors shape domestic policymaking. However, the effects of such domestic policy on foreign trading partners must be considered with greater sensitivity especially given increasing protectionistic pressures worldwide. It is insufficient to attempt to deflect foreign market access demands by pointing to domestic policy concerns. Japan has become too economically interdependent to continue to ignore foreign economic demands or interests. In order to maintain economic health Japan must now fully integrate the legitimate economic concerns of its trading partners into its domestic policy planning.

Perhaps Japan should take the lead internationally by proposing that protection of domestic markets should be permitted, but only up to an agreed upon level. Such a step would still permit domestic policy considerations for certain economic sectors, yet would limit the overall volume of protected activity and force trade-offs among domestic interest groups. It could go a long way toward increased transparency and the diffusion of trade tensions. Such a proposal could breathe new life into the GATT by permitting it, very much like arms control negotiations, to focus on a gradual reduction of the levels of protectionism over the years. It would also be preferable to the exchange of equivalent concessions which results only in a delay, not a resolution of disputes.

Obviously, there is not that much the Japanese government can do about the existence of close commercial relations between private corporations, either as *keiretsu* or looser groupings. Yet, to the extent that they result in more closed markets, it must do what little it can. It can at least ensure that these relations do not exceed the bounds set by national antitrust legislation and reinforce the Fair Trade Commission so that it becomes a more effective watchdog. Indeed, since some of these relations may hurt domestic consumers, it might consider the possibility of stricter rules in the national interest as well as that of international harmony.

Moreover, since its distribution system is more constricted by such commercial arrangements than that of many of its trading partners, Japan could think in terms of some form of compensation. It could take further measures to facilitate entry along the lines of the trade fairs and assistance provided by MIPRO, JETRO, and other bodies. At the very least, it should act swiftly to eliminate remaining tariffs, quotas, nontariff barriers, and administrative impediments since foreign companies will have to contend with the commercial barriers anyway.

Perceptions of the Japanese market is the second item the public sector must address. Often these perceptions matter just as much as, and sometimes more than, reality. Since negative beliefs about trading partners increase during periods of economic difficulties and large trade imbalances, it is vital that Japan address this issue rapidly.[3]

In particular, changes within the Japanese market will be insufficient if they are not communicated properly. Gradual dissemination of information may be too slow. Due to preconceived notions, Japanese trade relations may become aggravated to such an extent that actual changes will matter very little. For U.S. institutions and individuals, for example, the issue of fairness is very important. The perception of fairness is not achieved by the use of industry associations for certification or regulatory purposes. While this may be quite acceptable in Japan, and even though this process may run more smoothly if it is regulated by Japanese citizens only rather than by both Japanese and foreign citizens, it does create the impression of unfairness. Such an impression, regardless of its factual merits, will continue to hurt trading relations and must therefore be addressed. Similarly, announcements of market-opening efforts that do not describe at the same time the expected results, together with clear time delineations, will be ridiculed and dismissed as simple public relations tactics. In addition to the import imperative to be addressed by the private sector in Japan, the public sector must facilitate these imports and concurrently make major efforts to achieve international trade transparency.

POLICY BY TRADING PARTNERS

Foreign policymakers also have a responsibility to improve trade relations. With Japan they must develop a coherent and cohesive global trade strategy. United States trade officials, for example, cannot continue to trip over each other's luggage at Narita airport. The responsibility for trade policy must be unified and accorded the same national priority as any other $500 billion economic activity.

The United States must temper its desire for equal market access and demand and accept equivalent concessions across the board. Determining such equivalence, particularly for the longer run, requires detailed information. Once the bargaining chips have been determined, however, equivalence must be placed in the context of a time frame and revised periodically so that they result in a resolution rather than a delay of trade disputes.

United States policymakers, both Congress and the president and his staff, need to be realistic about their time frames. While deadlines must be set in order to achieve results, trade imbalances cannot be legislated away within a matter of days or weeks. Just as Japan's evolution from minor international player to trade superpower has not occurred overnight, the U.S trade deficit is not the result of short-term factors. To overcome problems such as the high value of the dollar, declines in the growth rate of productivity, the adversarial relationship between government and business and between business and labor, and the lack of international orientation on the part of U.S. firms, stop-gap solutions are insufficient. Such solutions would only result in a temporary "trade-managed" adjustment rather than successful market penetration abroad by U.S. firms. In order to locate receptive trading partners, the United States must match foreign concessions with policies to bring the domestic economic structure back in order, instead of offering market access concessions that are increasingly hard to find. In addition, if the U.S. public is to continue its free trade stance, it must also ask the private sector to share the burden. Industries that benefit from free trade policies must be willing and able to assist those industries, firms, and individuals that suffer from those policies.

On both sides of the Pacific, there is a need to eliminate the scapegoat mentality. The relationship, not only between Japan and the United States, but between all the countries globally tied to each other via the benefits of international trade, is far too important to become a sacrificial lamb on the altar of protectionism. We need to work together, acknowledging and respecting our cultural and societal differences. We need to begin talking with, not at, each other in order to promote change that is acceptable, tolerable, and beneficial for all participants. Trading nations no longer have regional or national markets. National economic and domestic policies are clearly only fractional components of our world trade framework, and will have to be subjugated to broader international considerations. This recognition must come about multilaterally, without scorn or ire, as an adaptation to new realities. Only then will it be possible to realize the benefits of a multilateral free trade system.

NOTES

1. Miroshi Sawana, "A Roundtable Discussion: Japan Moves to Encourage Manufactured Imports," *The Wheel Extended*, Special Supplement 7, Summer, 1980, pp. 2,7, as quoted by: Johnson Chalmers, "The Internationalization of the Japanese Economy," *California Management Review*, Vol. 25, No. 3, 1983.

2. Konaga Keiichi, "Future of Japan's Distribution Industry," *Dentsu Japan Marketing/Advertising*, Spring issue, Tokyo, 1984.

3. Mike Mansfield, "Address to the Foreign Correspondents Club of Japan," Tokyo, January 6, 1982.

Bibliography

BOOKS

Abegglen, James C. *The Strategy of Japanese Business.* Ballinger, Cambridge. 1984.

An Analysis of and Recommendations Regarding the Japanese Distribution System and Business Practices. Manufactured Imports Promotion Committee. Tokyo. 1983.

Antimonopoly Legislation of Japan. Edited by Counselor's Office of Fair Trade Commission, Kosei Torihiki Kyokai. 1977.

Blaker, Michael, ed. *The Politics of Trade: U.S. and Japanese Policymaking for the GATT Negotiations.* Columbia University Press, New York. 1978.

Bunge, Frederica M., ed. *Japan, a Country Study.* Foreign Area Studies, The American University. U.S. Government Printing Office. 1983.

CED, *Strategy for U.S. Industrial Competitiveness.* Committee for Economic Development. New York. 1984.

"Cracking The Japanese Market." Mainichi Daily News/Mainichi Newspapers, Tokyo, 1985.

Czinkota, Michael R. *Export Development Strategies.* Praeger, New York. 1982.

Czinkota, Michael R., and George Tesar, ed. *Export Management.* Praeger, New York. 1982.

De Mente, Boyd. *How to do Business in Japan.* Center for International Business. Los Angeles. 1972.

Dentsu Incorporated. *Marketing Opportunities in Japan.* McGraw-Hill Book Company (UK) Ltd. 1975.

Destler, I.M. and Sato, Hideo, eds. *Coping with U.S.-Japanese Economic Conflicts.* D.C. Heath, Lexington, Mass. 1982.

Distribution Systems in Japan. An Original Study. Business Intercommunications, Inc. Toyko. 1979.

Dodwell Marketing Consultants. *Industrial Groupings in Japan.* Tokyo 1984.

———. *Key Players in the Japanese Electronics Industry.* Tokyo, 1985.

———. *Retail Distribution in Japan.* Tokyo, 1985.

———. *The Structure of the Japanese Retail and Distribution Industry.* Tokyo. 1985.

_____ . *The Structure of the Japanese Auto Parts Industry*. Tokyo. 1983.
Henderson, Dan Fenno. *Foreign Enterprises in Japan*. Tuttle, Tokyo. 1975.
Higashi, Chikara. *Japanese Trade Policy Formulation*. Praeger, New York. 1983.
HI-OVIS Project. Final Report, Phase I Experiment. Published by Visual Information System Development Association. Tokyo. 1983.
Holloway, Robert J. and Nagashima, Akira. *Multinationals in Japan*. University of Minnesota. 1980.
Hufbauer, Gary; Czinkota, Michael R.; and Trozzo, Charles, eds. *U.S. International Economic Policy, 1981*. The International Law Institute. Washington, D.C. 1982.
Laumer, Helmut. *Die Warendistribution in Japan*. Institute Fuer Asienkunde. Hamburg. 1979.
Nakane, Chie. *Japanese Society*. Penguin Books. New York. 1981.
Pratt, Edward Ewing. *The Foreign Trade Handbook*. The Dartnell Corporation. Chicago. 1948.
Richardson, Bradley M. and Veda, Taizo, eds. *Business and Society in Japan, Fundamentals for Businessmen*. East Asian Studies Program, Ohio State University. Praeger, New York. 1981.
Selling Japan from A to Z. Edited by the Ministry of International Trade and Industry. Published by Manufactured Imports Promotion Organization. Tokyo.
Tokyo Keizai. *Japan Company Handbook*. Tokyo. Semi-Annual.
Tung, Rosalie L. *Business Negotiations with the Japanese*. Lexington Books. 1984.
Woronoff, Jon. *Inside Japan, Inc.* Lotus Press, Tokyo. 1982.
_____ . *World Trade War*. Praeger, New York. 1984.
Yamamura, Kozo, ed. *Policy and Trade Issues of the Japanese Economy*. University of Washington Press, Seattle. 1982.
Yoshihara, Junio. *Sogo Shosha*. Oxford University Press, Tokyo. 1982.
Young, Alexander K. *The Sogo Shosha: Japan's Multinational Trading Companies*. Westview Press, Boulder. 1979.
Zimmerman, Mark. *How to do Business with the Japanese*. Random House, New York. 1985.

REPORTS AND ARTICLES

Ahern, Raymond J. "Market Access in Japan: The U.S. Experience." Congressional Research Service. Report #85-37E, Feb. 14, 1985. Washington, D.C.

American Chamber of Commerce in Japan. "Report on Trade Barriers, Membership Survey." Tokyo. 1982.

Brock, William E. *Japanese Barriers to U.S. Trade and Recent Japanese Government Trade Initiatives.* Office of the United States Trade Representative. Washington, D.C. November, 1982.

_____ . "William E. Brock on International Trade." *The Brookings Review.* Spring, 1984.

Burton, Jack and Chase, Dennis. "Sun Still Not Shining on P&G in Japan." *Advertising Age.* December 20, 1982.

Businger, Donald. "Exports to Japan May Recover but Record U.S. Deficit is Likely." *Business America.* February 21, 1983.

Covey, Amanda. "Vertical Restraints Under Japanese Law." *Law in Japan.* Vol. 14, 1981.

Czinkota, Michael R. "Changes in the Japanese Distribution System for Consumer Products." Staff Paper #18, National Center for Export-Import Studies, Washington, D.C. 1985.

_____ . "Distribution of Consumer Products in Japan." *International Marketing Review.* Fall, 1985.

Czinkota, Michael R. "Distribution of Consumer Products in Japan: An Overview." Staff Paper #17, National Center for Export-Import Studies, Washington, D.C. 1985.

_____ . "Distribution in Japan: Problems and Changes." *Columbia Journal of World Business.* Fall, 1985.

_____ . "New GATT Round Needed Quickly." *Journal of Commerce.* June 21, 1985.

_____ . "Trade Sense, Not Sparks." *Japan Times.* April 29, 1985.

Czinkota, Michael R., and Kollmer, Paul. "U.S.-Japanese Trade Strategies." *Journal of Commerce.* May 13, 1985.

"Export-Import Bank Financing for Small Business." Hearing before the Subcommittee on Export Promotion and Market Development of the Committee on Small Business, United States Senate, Ninety-Eighth Congress, 1st Session. April 7, 1983.

"Export Promotion and Small Business." Hearing before the Subcommittee on Export Opportunities and Special Small Business Problems of the Committee on Small Business, House of Representatives, Ninety-Seventh Congress. September 21, 1982.

Fair Trade Commission. "The Fair Trade Commission's Approach to Trade Friction." April, 1983.

Haley, John O. "Marketing and Antitrust in Japan." *Hastings International and Comparative Law Review.* Vol. 2, No. 1, 1979.

"Helping High Tech Firms into the Japanese Market." *Business America.* July 25, 1983.

Hirotaka, Takeuchi and Bucklin, Louis P. "Productivity in Retailing: Retail Structure and Public Policy." *Journal of Retailing.* Vol. 53, No. 1, 1977.

_____. "In the Convenience Store Sector, Strategic Management is a Must." *Japan Times.* December, 1983.

Inako, T. "Culture in Business." *Journal of the ACCJ.* February, 1983.

Ishida, Hideto. "Anticompetitive Practices in the Distribution of Goods and Services in Japan: The Problems of Distribution Keiretsu." *Journal of Japanese Studies.* Vol. 9, No. 2, Summer, 1983.

"Japan and Korea." *Business America.* October 31, 1983.

"Japan Business, Obstacles, and Opportunities." Prepared by McKinsey and Company, Inc., for the United States-Japan Trade Study Group. 1983.

"Japan Opens its High-Tech Door a Little Wider." *Business Week.* February 6, 1984.

"Japanese Imports' Burden Eased." *Journal of Commerce.* November 16, 1983.

"The Japanese Non-Tariff Barrier Issue." National Institute for Research Advancement, Arthur D. Little, Tokyo. 1979.

Johannsson, Johnny K. and Ikujiro, Nonaka. "Japanese Exporting Marketing: Structures, Strategies, Counterstrategies." *International Marketing Review.* Vol. 1, No. 2, Winter, 1983.

Johnson, Chalmers. "The 'Internationalization' of the Japanese Economy." *California Management Review.* Vol. 25, No. 3, Spring, 1983. pp. 5–26.

Kanabayashi, Masayoshi. "Japan's Complex Distribution System Hinders Foreign Companies' Efforts to Sell Goods There." *Wall Street Journal.* May 3, 1978. p. 44.

Kearney International. "Non-Tariff Barriers Affecting the Health Care Industry in Japan." Tokyo. 1980.

"Keizai Koho Center, Japan 1983." Japan Institute for Social and Economic Affairs. Tokyo. 1983.

Konaga, Keiichi. "Future of Japan's Distribution Industry." *Dentsu Japan Marketing/Advertising.* Spring issue. p. 1

Lazer, William; Shoji, Murata; and Hiroshi, Kosaka. "Japanese Marketing: Towards a Better Understanding." *Journal of Marketing.* Vol. 49. No. 2, 1985.

Lohr, Steve. "U.S. Move Worries Japanese." *New York Times.* December 27, 1982. p. D1.

"Marketing in Japan." *Overseas Business Reports.* OBR–82. June, 1982.

McDermid, John F. "U.S.-Japan Trade: Problems and Prospects." *Fletcher Forum.* Vol. 7, No. 2, Summer, 1983. pp. 385–94.

Ministry of International Trade and Industry. "The Performance of Foreign-Affiliated Companies." Annual.

_____. "White Paper on International Trade, 1983." Tokyo. 1983.

Nagashima, Akira. "A Comparative 'Made In' Product Image Survey Among Japanese Businessmen." *Journal of Marketing*. July, 1977. pp. 95–100.

––––––. "A Comparison of Japanese and U.S. Attitudes Towards Foreign Products." *Journal of Marketing*. Vol. 34, January, 1970. pp. 68–74.

"Obstacles to Exporting Faced by Small Business." Hearing before the Committee on Small Business, United States Senate, Ninety-Eighth Congress, 1st Session. February 11, 1983.

O'Neill, Robert. "Go West Young Man—To Japan?" *Progressive Grocer*. January, 1984. pp. 7, 10.

"Outline of Japanese Distribution Structures." The Distribution Economics Institute of Japan. Published by the Nihon Keizai Shimbum. 1973–74 Enlarged Edition.

"Penetrating the Japanese Market." Committee for Manufactured Goods Import Measures, Manufactured Imports Promotion Organization. No. 3. July, 1980.

Ross, Randolph E. "Understanding the Japanese Distribution System: An Explanatory Framework." *European Journal of Marketing*. Vol. 17, No. 1, 1983.

"Seibu Considering Flexible Job Program." *Japan Times*. March 10, 1984.

The Seibu Group, 1984, Annual Report. Tokyo. 1984.

Shimaguchi, Mitsuaki and Lazer, William. "Japanese Distribution Channels: Invisible Barriers to Market Entry." *MSU Business Topics*. Vol. 27, No. 1, 1970.

Shimaguchi, Mitsuaki and Rosenberg, Larry J. "Demystifying Japanese Distribution." *Columbia Journal of World Business*. Spring, 1979.

"Strategies for Alleviating Recurrent Bilateral Trade Problems Between Japan and the United States." *The Japanese Non-Tariff Trade Barrier Issue: American Views and Implications for Japan-U.S. Trade Relations*. Report to the Japanese National Institute for Research Advancement. Arthur D. Little, Inc. May, 1979.

Tabner, Jody. "Lagging Recovery in Japan Adds to Record U.S. Deficit." *Business America*. Vol. 6, No. 17, August 22, 1983.

"Today's Challenge to American Business School Education." Business Schools' Deans Conference. The White House. The United States Department of Commerce and U.S.-Japan Communication. 1983.

"Trade Between Japan and the United States." The Boston Consulting Group, Tokyo. April 14, 1978.

Tsuji, Yoshihiko. "Regulation of Resale Price Maintenance In Japan." *New York Law Forum.* Vol. 18, No. 2, 1972.

Tsurumi, Yoshi. "Managing Consumer and Industrial Systems in Japan." *Sloan Management Review.* Fall, 1982.

"The United Kingdom Market for Machine Tools." Prepared for the Japan Trade Center. London. December, 1983.

"U.S., Japan, Europe Sign Agreement of Patent Cooperation." *Business America.* October 31, 1983.

United States Congress. Hearings before the Committee on Foreign Affairs, House of Representatives. March-August, 1982. Washington, D.C. U.S. Government Printing Office.

Weil, Frank A. and Glick, Norman D. "Japan--Is the Market Open?" *Law and Policy in International Business.* Vol. 11, No. 3, 1979.

Willoughby, David G. "Adopting Successfully to the Japanese Market." *Journal of the ACCJ.* June, 1981.

JETRO MATERIALS

"Comparison Between the United Kingdom and Japan on the Distribution of Machine Tools and Suggestions." Overseas Economic Information Center.

"Doing Businss in Japan." Marketing Series 8. Tokyo. Revised 1982.

"Foreign Companies in Japan." *Now in Japan,* No. 33, 1982.

Ichihashi, Tatsuhiko. "Hang in There! How to Sell in the Japanese Market." Delivered at the JETRO Business Round Table Meeting, Tokyo. September 21, 1982. *Speaking of Japan.* March, 1983.

"Improvements of Japan's Standards and Certification Systems." Special Report. July, 1983.

"Inside the Japanese Market for Manufactured Imports." Tokyo. 1983.

"Japan as an Export Market." Marketing Series 1. Tokyo. Revised 1983.

"The Japanese Consumer." Marketing Series 6. Tokyo. Revised 1983.

"Japanese Market-Opening and Import Promotion Measures." Information File 4. February, 1984.

"Japan's Import and Marketing Regulations—Selected Consumer Products." Marketing Series 11. Tokyo. Revised 1980.

"Market for Machine Tools in Japan." Overseas Economic Information Center. January, 1984.

"Marketing and Distribution Strategies of Foreign Products in Japan." Tokyo. Undated.

"Passenger Automobile Market in Japan." Overseas Economic Information Center. January, 1984.

"Planning for Distribution in Japan." Marketing Series 5. Revised 1980.

"Sales Promotion in the Japanese Market." Marketing Series 7. Tokyo. revised 1983.

"Softnomics." Tokyo. 1984.

Index

About The Authors

MICHAEL R. CZINKOTA is chairman of the National Center for Export-Import Studies at Georgetown University, where he is also a member of the faculty of marketing and international business. He studied law and business administration at the University of Erlangen-Nuernberg in West Germany and was a partner in an export-import firm. In 1975 he won a Fulbright Award and studied at Ohio State University, where he received his M.B.A. in 1976 and his Ph.D. in 1980. Dr. Czinkota has written extensively on the subject of international trade in publications such as *Columbia Journal of World Business* and *Journal of International Business Studies.* His most recent books are *Export Policy, Export Management, Export Development Strategies, US-Arab Economic Relations, US-Latin American Trade Relations* and *Export Controls.*

JON WORONOFF has more than a decade's experience of dealing with Japan, first as a businessman and then as a business journalist. He ran a small company and acted as consultant for other foreign companies during the mid-1970s. More recently, he covered the business scene for several leading Asian publications. In the course of these activities, he experienced the difficulties of doing business in Japan and studied the problems encountered by many companies in assorted sectors. Woronoff has written numerous articles on trade conflicts for such publications as *Asian Business, Modern Asia, Oriental Economist, Japan Economic Journal,* and *Mainichi Daily News.* He has also produced books on significant aspects of Japanese business and economics, including *Japan: The Coming Economic Crisis, Japan's Commercial Empire, The Japan Syndrome,* and *World Trade War.*

About The National Center For Export-Import Studies

The National Center for Export-Import Studies (NCEIS) was founded by Dr. Michael R. Czinkota in 1981 at Georgetown University to provide international trade analysis and information, and to strengthen communication among the business, policy, and academic sectors of the international trade community. NCEIS is a nonprofit organization.

NCEIS identifies and investigates trends in world trade and devises forward-looking commercial strategies for the United States, its businesses, and its trading partners. The Center also monitors current trade events and produces relevant and timely analyses.

NCEIS maintains the philosophy that open, multilateral trade is essential to global prosperity. It encourages the development of free-trade policies and acceptable business practices through editorials, position papers, congressional testimony, and its publication, *The Trade Analyst*. In doing so, NCEIS maintains no political affiliations and strives to be nonpartisan in its work.

In addition to its research and communication activities, the Center is a leading force in international business education. NCEIS offers trade education courses for business executives and government officials who wish to increase their understanding of the mechanisms, regulations, and policy issues involved in the conduct of world trade. The Center also offers specialized personnel-training programs for private sector firms. NCEIS also maintains created a prototype export trading company to provide hands-on understanding of the necessary steps for successful internationalization of business activities.